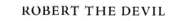

ROBERT THE DEVIL

Chi comence li Romans de Robert
le diable. Las qui vous ores et suir

r entendes gnr z menor
adis al tans ancienor
uot i due en normendie
out bien z drois qie n die
p rendome ert z de gru lignage
fu auoit ml baselage
ffes estoit haus hon z prous
e ses armes cheualerous
i baron de si duchere
f print de son millor de
i lorent si cheualier
el pleist feme z mollier
i dus bonement sor orfie
cil se misent ala voie
r uous feroie pl loue ere
ne puchele fille i are
i oit si baro amesle
el i apiele z espouse
e lignage z gru akme
ele z gentilg z de boinane
l e noches en furent ml riches
d ssed ior gres z puinches
a ffes dona li dus argent
a f iogleres z a autre gent
i dus i la ducoisse ensamble
urent longant che me samble

Gl il onqs enfant ne norent
ft e qi ml auoir ne poient
p or promesse ne por preyere
el o dieu feissoit ne ast piere
d lun z lautre furent coste
f l auient apres pentecoste
t i queuo ala au bos cachier
u n cerf passlent li leuirer
l a duchoisse ale cuer dolant
el le ne par auoir enfant
d eu fait ele ome hteo
el gnit doner ne uie auleo
u ne eueue non poissant
d ones uous sire teus enfant
f moi sire qi tant ai auoir
t e puis che nist uio ml auoir
El por q ml poor ayeo
el uous sire ml ure doneo
d iable fait ele ie te pri
el en enteuqes ia un nuit
S e tu me dones si gisant
c he te pri des ore en drant
t ant emes for le ht pasmee
al releuier soit ml islamee
ay aus li dus en meslue teus
e e diacher uient pl nedauene
d sst en la sale amont pureo
e es ses uesses sest desauches
ure en la chambre dou pure
l iene ala mollier trouee
i dus regarde sa biaute
eos se li pluist tel uolente
d cloi ... dalui pesar
t aut en ot li dus gru destir
el il tarpoire for son ht
El lis tant isst mal se duit

ROBERT *the* DEVIL

The First Modern English Translation

of *Robert le Diable*, an Anonymous French

Romance of the Thirteenth Century

PREPARED BY SAMUEL N. ROSENBERG

The Pennsylvania State University Press
University Park, Pennsylvania

The manuscript of the underlying Old French text of *Robert le Diable* is in the Bibliothèque nationale de France (MS BnF fr. 25516).

This translation uses the critical edition of the Old French text prepared by Eilert Löseth: *Robert le Diable: Roman d'aventures*, Société des Anciens Textes Français (Paris: Firmin Didot, 1903).

Library of Congress Cataloging-in-Publication Data

Names: Rosenberg, Samuel N., translator.
Title: Robert the devil : the first modern English translation of Robert le diable, an anonymous French romance of the thirteenth century / Prepared by Samuel N. Rosenberg.
Other titles: Roman de Robert le Diable. English.
Description: University Park, Pennsylvania : The Pennsylvania State University Press, [2018] | "This translation uses the critical edition of the Old French text prepared by Eilert Löseth; Robert le diable: roman d'aventures, Société des anciens textes français (Paris: Firmin Didot, 1903)."—Title page verso. | Includes bibliographical references and index.
Summary: "English translation of an anonymous thirteenth-century French poem in which a woman desperate to bear a child appeals to the devil for help. Originally written in octosyllabic rhymed couplets, this translation uses free verse"—Provided by publisher.
Identifiers: LCCN 2017035792 | ISBN 9780271080161 (pbk. : alk. paper)
Subjects: | LCGFT: Free verse.
Classification: LCC PQ1516.R7 R67 2018 | DDC 841/.1—dc23
LC record available at https://lccn.loc.gov/2017035792

The Pennsylvania State University Press is a member of the Association of American University Presses.

It is the policy of The Pennsylvania State University Press to use acid-free paper. Publications on uncoated stock satisfy the minimum requirements of American National Standard for Information Sciences—Permanence of Paper for Printed Library Material, ANSI Z39.48-1992.

Frontispiece: Anonymous, *Beuve of Hantone; Elijah of Saint-Gille; Aiol; Robert the Devil* 1275–90, fol. 174r. Bibliothèque nationale de France, D'epartement des manuscrits, Francais 25516. Photo: BnF.

CONTENTS

ACKNOWLEDGMENTS

I would like to extend my sincere thanks to my
colleague Logan Whalen, the staff of Pennsylvania
State University Press, the Press's anonymous
readers, my friends, and my family for their many
and varied contributions.

I dedicate this translation, with love, to my husband,
Jeffrey S. Ankrom.

INTRODUCTION

Robert le Diable—an anonymous French *roman d'aventures*—has roots no doubt going down into preliterate, pre-Christian folkloric materials, for an account of human birth through divine or supernatural agency is clearly not an invention of the European Middle Ages.[1] As fully recounted for the first time in a manuscript of the thirteenth century and provided with a historically and geographically plausible setting, it is basically the tale of a boy born to a childless noble couple only after the mother has secretly called on Satan to help her conceive. The behavior of the boy, and then of the strong, powerfully built young man skilled at arms that he becomes, is so destructive and brutal that one day, loathing himself, he prevails on his mother to reveal the secret of his birth and thus the source of his wickedness. He leaves his home in Normandy, as well as his privileged position as the only child of the Duke, to seek salvation in Rome. The Pope and then a pious hermit set him on the way to remission of his sins through a lengthy, arduous penance, whose most striking requirement is that he never speak. Living dumbly at the Roman court as the Emperor's pet fool, Robert becomes aware of a Turkish threat of·invasion. He prays to God to allow him to use his ever-extraordinary strength and fighting ability to help the Romans, though without revealing his identity. Thanks to an angelic emissary of the Lord, Robert is able to accomplish his desired mission. The Saracens are persistent enemies, however, and it is only after three successive military campaigns that they are finally defeated, the Romans all the while wondering who their elusive champion might be. Robert's identity has been known all along to the Emperor's daughter but has remained a secret, because she, like Robert, is mute (but for nonpenitential reasons). Dramatic events, involving a villainous seneschal rejected as a suitor to the Princess, ultimately restore the power of speech to both Robert and the Emperor's daughter. The Emperor, grateful for Robert's decisive help against the Turks, wishes to grant him his very willing daughter in marriage. Robert declines, however, and returns to the hermit's abode, where his path to salvation began. When Robert dies, he is venerated as a saint.

The tale touches on a remarkably broad range of medieval concerns, from genealogy and the shaping of character to all the manifestations, implications, and effects of transgression. The problem of sin, personal responsibility, and penitence is a central issue, as is the transformation of an outsized epic warrior into a self-effacing saint. The nested questions of divine justice, pontifical authority, the penitential value of silence and anonymity, and eremitic charity are essential to the unfolding of the story, but no element of the legend could be more excitingly central than the all-consuming conflict between Christendom and the Muslim world in these days of an ongoing Crusade. Along the way, the narrative provides engaging insights into the mores of the papal court in Rome, from the seating of the various diners at a banquet and the polite order of hand washing to the treatment of a disabled princess and the early employment of sign language.

The romance has come down to us in 5,078 lines of rhymed octosyllabic couplets, transmitted (along with three other romances) in a manuscript from the second half of the thirteenth century, fr. 25516 of the Bibliothèque nationale de France.[2] Large, colored capital letters open the various sections of the manuscript; these are represented in our transcription by large capital letters. There is a second redaction, somewhat different and slightly briefer, preserved in a manuscript of the late fourteenth or early fifteenth century, BnF fr. 24405. The first of these versions (A), published in Eilert Löseth's unsurpassed critical edition of 1903, is the text that underlies our English translation, as it does the modern French translation by Alexandre Micha. The second version (B) is the basis for Élisabeth Gaucher's edition and modern French translation (see the bibliography).[3]

LATER VERSIONS

The tale of Robert the Devil is clearly a gripping story, for very soon after the writing of version A, it was worked into a Latin *exemplum* in Lyon by the Dominican monk Étienne de Bourbon. It appeared in the decade of the 1250s in his *Tractatus de divesis materiis predicabilibus* as an abridged retelling, the didactic purpose of which was to demonstrate the beneficent effects of penance.

This version was followed by another pious treatment in Latin, notably as an *exemplum* cited by the Dominican Jean Gobi in his *Scala coeli* for its lesson in the appeasement of divine wrath. Gobi's version was still used by Franciscan preachers in southern Italy at the end of the fifteenth century.[4]

A short version of the legend was transmitted in the thirteenth century in the first *Chronique de Normandie*, an anonymous Norman history in French prose. This was succeeded around the middle of the following century by a longer version, attributed to one Anonyme de Béthune. The unknown author of this rewriting, called the *Grande Chronique de Normandie*, was probably a native of Normandy or Picardy.[5]

The appeal of the story remained powerful. If the *Grande Chronique* relates it as a sort of history, the equally anonymous *Dit de Robert le Diable*, composed in the first half of the fourteenth century, appears to have made use of it for moral instruction. In this instance, version A of the tale was condensed into a sequence of 254 quatrains of monorhymed alexandrines.[6]

Further rewritngs, with a significant change of genre, also appeared in the fourteenth century. In two notable cases, adaptation of the legend entailed a move to the dramatic stage. There is, first, an anonymous *mystère*, the scenic details of which are not known, but a modern French adaptation of it, written by the historian Édouard Fournier, was performed in 1878 and published in the following year. The American poet W. S. Merwin later wrote an English translation of the French adaptation.[7]

The other fourteenth-century rewriting for the theater is the *Miracle de Robert le Diable*, number 33 in the forty-piece collection of *Miracles de Notre Dame par personnages*, a play apparently performed between 1339 and 1350 by and for the Confrérie Saint-Éloi, the guild of goldsmiths of Paris; the unknown author, no doubt of Norman or Picard origin, based his text on the *Dit de Robert le Diable*.[8]

The legend of Robert the Devil entered the age of printing in 1496, when the *Dit de Robert le Diable* was rewritten in Lyon as a prose text, called *La Vie du terrible Robert le Diable*. Between that date and 1580, eleven editions reproduced the same text, including seven in Paris, with a total printing of more than a thousand copies.[9] This prose text was the model for the version that came to be sold in the following century in the Bibliothèque Bleue.

The creation of the Bibliothèque Bleue in the early 1600s led to a proliferation of chapbooks throughout France. Right through the following two centuries, the prose *Vie de Robert le Diable* remained a best seller, prized for its tale of chivalric prowess in the face of a faithless foe, a touchingly chaste love, and, no doubt particularly, moral edification, especially as a complement to the preaching of small-town and rural clergy.[10]

In the latter part of the eighteenth century, the scholarly journalist Jean de Castilhon composed a new, augmented version of the legend, with various new episodes and commentary, intended for a more sophisticated readership. Published in 1769 and then reprinted, it was released in 1784 in a condensed version meant, again, for an upper-class public, the contemporary bourgeoisie. Castilhon's new conception of the story entails considerable ideological, cultural, and narrative updating. This is no small shift from the medieval tale of version A.[11]

Numerous editions and revisions followed in the nineteenth century, with notable efforts to counteract the would-be modernizing tendencies of Castilhon and revert to the alleged naive and wholesome simplicity of the original legend. Such efforts, located within the Nouvelle Bibliothèque Bleue, were led by the influential Romantic writer Charles Nodier and supported by the extensive philological and historical work of Antoine Le Roux de Lincy.

Surely, the most startling remaking of the tale in the nineteenth century came in the form of an adaptation for the operatic stage. This was the work of the composer Giacomo Meyerbeer and the very well-known Parisian playwright-librettist Eugène Scribe. Their groundbreaking grand opera, produced for the first time in 1831, had an unprecedented success, with further stagings in the same decade not only in European cities but in the Americas as well, including New York, New Orleans, and Mexico City. Numerous critics, French and foreign, were quick to voice enthusiastic approval and disapproval, but performances long remained a staple of the Paris Opéra, the most recent production being a brilliant revival in 1985. The Romantic tale presented by Meyerbeer and Scribe is an adaptation of the legend unimaginable in earlier years, yet, in retrospect, understandable as a further refashioning in a long line of attempts to make a new use of age-old material.[12] Various cinematic treatments of the legend have also appeared in France and elsewhere.[13]

The legend of Robert the Devil, immensely popular in late medieval France, spread quite early to Spain and eventually to the Netherlands, Germany, and Italy. In fourteenth-century England, the unknown writer of *Sir Gowther* turned the tale into a metrical romance, and other English adaptations, by Wynkyn de Worde and by Thomas Lodge, appeared in the sixteenth century. In the twentieth century, as mentioned earlier, the poet W. S. Merwin published an English translation of a fourteenth-century French stage version of the legend.[14]

THE TRANSLATION

This is the first translation of the thirteenth-century French work into modern

English, done from the critical edition prepared by Eilert Löseth for the Société des Anciens Textes Français, published in 1903. The five thousand verses of Old French text, presented by its editor in numbered lines of rhymed octosyllabic couplets, appear in the present translation with Löseth's line numbering. The section divisions usually repeat those of the edited text, with the major difference that all passages of dialogue in the translation are preceded and followed by spaces to make the story easier to follow. The translation is in free, rhythmic verse, carrying a narrative meant to convey, like the original, the rhythm of a reciting voice. Indeed, the goal in the translation, as it was in the original text, is to create a work suitable for recitation, a work whose rhythms and sonorities bespeak the presence, now even on paper, of a storyteller. English lending itself much less readily than French to sustained rhyming, the translation has rhyme and assonance appearing regularly only in the final couplets of key sections and passages of dialogue. Elsewhere, there is abundant use of alliteration and of other homophonic echoes. Note that the narration includes many insertions by the jongleur; some are mere phrases, while others are extended remarks. In any case, the jongleur's presence through the text is an inescapable fact. The translated text, like the manuscript and the edited French text, does not signal the jongleur's insertions typographically.

Lexical choices inevitably include terms that are obviously congruent with the medieval subject matter, but they avoid vocabulary that is gratuitously quaint or archaic. The effort throughout is to offer a smoothly resonant English text that recounts its medieval tale in fittingly modern language.

NOTES

1. See the works of Thompson, notably his *Motif-Index of Folk-Literature*. Gaucher briefly discusses motivically related works in medieval French narratives in her *Robert le Diable: Histoire*, 42–46.

2. At the time of this writing, a digital image of the full manuscript can be consulted online and downloaded for personal study, at no cost, through the Gallica website of the Bibliothèque nationale de France (www.gallica.fr). One can search for manuscript 25516, in which this romance appears on folios 174r–209v. A usable Web address for the first leaf is http://gallica.bnf.fr/ark:/12148/btv1b84516032/f353.image; readers can navigate from there.

3. Gaucher points out in *Robert le Diable: Histoire* that it is hard to say whether version *B* is a rewriting of *A* or the reproduction of an early draft of the original. She goes on to summarize the differences between the two versions (21).

4. Ibid., 99–101; see also Andries, "Bibliothèque Bleue."

5. Gaucher, *Robert le Diable: Histoire*, 101–5; see also Andries, "Bibliothèque Bleue."

6. Gaucher, *Robert le Diable: Histoire*, 105–11; see also Andries, "Bibliothèque Bleue."

7. Merwin's source, the fourteenth-century play, had been published in *Le Mystère de Robert le Diable mis en deux parties avec transcription en vers modernes en regard du texte du XIV* siècle*, adapted and introduced by Édouard Fournier (Paris: Dentu, 1879). On the staging of 1878, see Castellani, "*Mystère de Robert le Diable.*"

8. Gaucher, *Robert le Diable: Histoire*, 111–27, presents an extensive treatment of the source manuscript, a detailed comparison of the dramatic text with the *Dit de Robert le Diable*, and, most interesting, an attempt to understand how the play may have been staged.

9. Ibid., 134; Timelli, Ferrari, and Schoysman, *Pour un nouveau répertoire*, 245–56.

10. Gaucher, *Robert le Diable: Histoire*, 134–81. See also the expanded study by Andries, *Dix-huitième siècle*.

11. Gaucher, *Robert le Diable: Histoire*, 134–81; Andries, *Dix-huitième siècle*. See also Trocquenet, "Réécriture de *Robert le Diable.*"

12. Gaucher, *Robert le Diable: Histoire*, 148–55; see also Clark, "Diable improbablement," and Clark, "Raising the Devil."

13. Gaucher, *Robert le Diable: Histoire*, 159.

14. See the extensive bibliographies in Gaucher, *Robert le Diable: Édition bilingue.*

ROBERT THE DEVIL

ROBERT THE DEVIL

N ow hear this, young and old:
Once there was, in days gone by,
A noble duke in Normandy
Whose tale it's fit to tell you.
A worthy man was he, well-born   5
And prized for bravery, for courage,
A man of high repute and honor,
Valiant at arms and chivalrous.
Once he'd reached the proper age,
The barons of his duchy   10
Urged him, good knight that he was,
To find a wife and marry.
Graciously, the Duke said yes,
And his aides began their quest.

But why prolong the story?   15
The barons found him a maiden,
Daughter of a noble count;
She came of high and honored birth
And was lovely, gracious, and kind.
The Duke soon took her as his lawful spouse.   20
Their nuptials were a splendid fete,
With counts and great lords in attendance;
The Duke lavished silver and gold
On singers, jugglers, and tales new told.

Duke and duchess, I've heard,   25
Lived together as man and wife should,

But no child ever came of their union.
Nothing they did would avail them that gift,
No promise, no prayer, and no pledge
To God or Saint Peter—no oath;   30
And a sorrow it was to them both.

It happened a while after Pentecost
The Duke was away in the woods,
Hunting with his hounds and tracking a stag.
The Duchess, heavyhearted at home,   35
Was lamenting how childless she was.

"God, you must hate me!" she cried.
"Fruitless is how you want me to be!
To a powerless pauper, good Lord,
You will give a child in no time,   40
While I, who have riches and wealth,
It seems clear, must live on deprived.
What a powerless God you are, Lord,
Unable to grant what I ask." She paused.
"Satan," she cried, "help me, I pray!   45
Henceforth my wish is addressed only to you.
Hear my plea and vouchsafe my desire!
Grant me a child!"

T hen she fell back on her bed in a faint.
      Later awake, in her heart she felt stained.   50

Meanwhile, the Duke, at the very same time,
Tired of hunting, returned to the castle.
He climbed up the stairs;
He took off his boots;
He walked into a chamber curtained in silk   55
And there found the Duchess, his wife.
The Duke gazed at her beauty
And was seized by desire to have her,
To lie with her, hold her close, hold her tight;
His need was great and could brook no delay;   60

No word did he utter as she lay there in bed,
He rushed and thrust until he was spent.

Alas! The seed he planted that day
Would yield in the Duchess such fruit,
Such an heir as they both would regret,   65
For that boy would bring no joy to the pair.
The Devil, who knew what he wanted,
Arranged it all to his liking.
So there's what you have: a child in the womb
But a mother in torment and sorrow,   70
Knowing full well it was no gift of God
And this birth would produce nothing good.

Her term approaching and time drawing near,
The hapless mother of the child to be
Could mutter despair to none but herself.   75
Everyone knew, far and wide through the land,
She was bearing a child, and soon it was due.
No one knew or could even believe
That soon there'd be war, though I have no doubt;
The child would strive hard to bring it about.   80

But now listen! The moment came
When the Duchess's labor began.
For the child, who made her suffer great pain,
Her labor was long, for it lasted a week,
With no sleep in that time, no rest or repose.   85
She brought forth a son, an ill-fated event!
Very soon, in good time,
The Duke's bishops all gathered
To give his name to the boy.
"Robert" they chose and thought well of their choice.   90

Now baptized, the boy, still wet
With water and salt and consecrated chrism,
Was handed to nurses to be nourished and fed.
But he was already so wicked, so ill-willed

And malignant, so determined to harm,   95
That no caress, no embrace could content him;
He refused to cease, at whatever hour, refused
To stop, day or night, his insistent cries.
Not for feeding or nursing, for pap or the breast,
Would he silence his tireless brawl;   100
He brayed like a beast; he barked like a dog.
He went on behaving like that,
Always angry and vicious,
Always hitting and kicking,
And whenever the devil went to the breast,   105
He would scratch and would bite.
He howled all the time and threatened to spit;
He couldn't keep still and not shout.
So fearful of him were his nurses,
Each so afraid to give him her breast,   110
They made a tube for his feeding,
To keep him as removed as they could.
They trembled, each one, lest he bite
When they attempted to lift him,
And if he didn't bite them or scratch,   115
He used his feet to hurt with a kick.
Robert, in fact, was unable to behave;
Always, he inclined to wound and torment.
He grew in one day
More than other children in seven.   120
But so beautiful a child was he
That at fourteen years old, it was clear
No lad could be more handsome than Robert,
More alert, more attractive, more glowing.
Once sure of his footing and able to run,   125
He became more a tyrant than ever;
He threw benches and stools
At his nurses and maids.
Once he could walk and could run,
He'd gather dirt through the palace   130
And throw it with straw at whoever stood near.
If a knight chanced to yawn,

He would stuff ash in his mouth
And would then run away.
They tried to teach him to read,   135
But no tutor could manage the task,
Not one or two or even three or four,
However much they threatened him and swore.

When he reached the age of fifteen,
There was no teacher, however well known,   140
With courage enough to come to the court,
For once Robert had him at hand,
He could rip him apart right down to his feet.
And if he protested even ever so little,
He might tear out both eyes   145
Or do to his body other such harm.
No priest and no cleric, even ordained,
However daring or bold,
Would not, if seen in the palace by Robert,
Have given all his gold to be elsewhere,   150
All the best gold to be found anywhere,
Lest, with whatever club might come to his hand,
The boy strike him harsh blows on the head.
Ah, God! How many a man of importance
Lost his life at the hands of that brute!   155
That, though, was hardly the worst,
For in church or in chapel
He could see no crystal or glass too lovely
To smash at one blow
And then run away.   160
Ah, but the poor! He detested the poor!
He couldn't find a single pauper
He wouldn't slay or strike or maim.
The Duchess heard their moans,   165
And the Duke, their distress;
The parents' pain was acute, their horror as well,
For they saw their son going down into Hell.

R obert grew, grew strong and grew tall—
  A growth that was grievous to many a man;   170
They would have preferred that he shrink,
That his strength lessen and vanish.
When Robert turned twenty years old,
No man could be found anywhere near,
However big and bold, I'd say,   175
Who, compared with the boy,
Would not be short by a foot.
Robert was bigger and stronger, more robust
Than anyone else born of woman.
Such was his destiny, such was his fate.   180
Wherever it was people gathered,
He could seize the most rugged of men
And readily bear them far from the start,
Such wondrous strength and power were his.
But, too, he was radiantly handsome,   185
Beautiful in face as he was in physique.
So it was stunning to see what evil could come
From a man so charming to all.
But no hermit there was, no priest or monk,
However good or decent he might be,   190
Whom he was not ready to slay on first sight,
And many were those he'd have killed
Had they not fled from the threat
As soon as his name had been uttered.
Monks ran from Robert; lay brothers, too;   195
And oh! Were they right to fear him and run!
The Pope in Rome was not amused,
But damned the man and denied him communion.
His father, the Duke, when he saw
That the son would accomplish no good,   200
Drove him far from the palace
And forth from his land;
He took care that he never return,
For the ill he might do, the harm and the hurt.

R obert saw he was hated by all 205
And that everyone cursed him.
He took off. He set out on the road,
Then found his way into the forest,
The forest that lies between Rouen and the Seine.
Soon he was leading a great band of robbers 210
And brigands and thieves.
He enjoyed such companions,
And with so many beside him,
He could do harm wherever he wished,
Which he proceeded to do. 215
He combed through highways and footpaths,
Searching along the way
For pilgrims and merchants.
No man could escape being caught;
Many were slain, some to flames promptly tossed. 220

M any, then, were Robert's wicked deeds.
Even before the year was past,
His men had set fire to abbeys and granges
And forced their people to scatter.
Any lady or maiden who fell across his path, 225
Whatever small hint of beauty she had,
Was swept without warning
Into Robert's fearsome embrace.
Word of his deeds reached his father, the Duke
And the Duchess, his mother. 230
Victims cried out for help.
From the Duke they received his oath
That, by God, he would drown him forthwith
If he but had him in hand.

"Have pity, my lord!" cried the Duchess. 235
"If you but wish, you can silence this clamor
In no time at all
With no drowning or death of whatever sort.
Raise our son to the rank of a knight
And then you will see him withdraw 240

Very soon from his life of misdeeds;
He will abandon his wicked, cruel ways;
His brutal behavior will be all set right—
Once you'll have made him a knight."

C ounsel like this the Duke found not unwelcome.   245
Early next morning, once he was up,
His messengers left in search of his son.
They turned right, they turned left,
Until, deep in the woods,
They found Robert, haranguing his troops.   250
He'd be knighted, he was told,
Once he'd returned to his family's fold.

H earing this message,
Robert was elated and thrilled.
He took leave of his thieves and other companions   255
And turned back, turned home, to the palace.
He rode into Rouen and strode into the court.
No man referred to his wayward life;
No one received him with either smiles or disdain.
His father, however, embraced him with warmth   260
And announced he would dub him a knight
If he abandoned his wicked behavior.
Robert made no protest but forthwith agreed,
So the promise of knighthood was now a done deed.

T his was the eve of Pentecost.   265
Like it or not, whatever one's wish,
Robert was now a new knight.
Arms and chargers and everyday horses
He gave right and left to gain love and his favor.
At Argences all was honor and feasting,   270
Festive music and pleasure.
He gave away silver, handed out gold;
To musicians and servants
He gave generous presents and gifts.
At the end of the party,   275

They set a date for a tourney
At Brittany's Mont-Saint-Michel.
Robert rode there in pomp,
Attended by knights and two hundred squires.
That's when began   280
The destructive exploits
That ravaged many a castle.
Robert, who had no wish to tarry,
Sought immediate lodgings,
Then spent the night awake in jubilation;   285
Never had he shown such ready expectation.

Next day, in the dawn's early light,
    Robert set out for the tourney,
Refusing, however, to start with a prayer
At chapel or church;   290
Some thought it wrong and called for rebuke,
But Robert didn't give a boiled egg for God's help;
He headed straight for the tourney.
No one, I think, has ever seen
A more memorable meet.   295
Right from the start, Robert sent
Fear and cold fright all through the ranks
With his unholy blows and harsh strikes.
He encountered no knight, however adept,
Whether head-on or coming up from the side,   300
Whom he failed to unhorse and throw to the ground.
As in a war to actual death,
Robert paused over every man down,
Ready to cut off his head.
No knight had the strength or the skill   305
To remain upright and elude the slash of his sword.
He disturbed the whole tourney,
Wrought destruction and havoc all through the field.
All the knights who were there swore to God
That they'd never again, as long as they lived,   310
Whatever the pleas, the promises or prayers,
Partake in a tourney

Where their foe would be Robert.
Nothing and no one did they hate with such rage;
No man did they dread as they dreaded him; 315
He panicked and frightened them all.
Robert went riding through Brittany,
Through France and through Lorraine.
Wherever he went, jousting came to a halt
And everything ground to a painful stop. 320
Robert, of course, was part of the cause,
But cowardice, too, gave many men pause.

Once tourneys were over,
Robert, who had caused so much ill,
Turned back to Normandy. 325
In every place where he stayed,
He caused trouble beyond all accounting.
But friars and clergy were particular targets,
And on them he inflicted unspeakable crimes.
Such was Robert's diabolic behavior 330
That no God-fearing person remained there,
For everyone fled at his merest approach.
There was hardly a man dared come near him;
Every squire and guard was frightened and feared him.

Then it happened one day 335
He was staying in the castle of Arques,
Where the Duchess had come
And the Duke had held court.
Robert, who was loath to do good,
Imagined a plan to do ill. 340
He rode up to an abbey
That, with barons and household retainers,
Housed five dozen nuns.
With one hand alone he choked
The fifty most appealing of all. 345
He put every breast to the sword;
He slaughtered and slew,
Then ran a torch through the street,

Burned down their quarters and set stables ablaze,
Just as the Devil dictated.   350
By the time he was finished, exhausted and listless,
The nuns were all slain, none left to bear witness.

Once he had done this, he rode off
    On his horse, whose whinnies and snorts
Sounded all through the forest.   355
He spurred and prodded and pricked
Until he was back at the castle of Arques.
He looked a hideous sight,
But no one was there to see or to greet him.
Robert dismounted and glanced all around;   360
He looked up and down and throughout;
He looked to the right, he looked to the left;
Nowhere, however, was man or woman to be seen.
He shouted for his squire
To come take his horse,   365
But it took a long while
For the man to appear,
So fearful, like all, to be anywhere near.

Robert was plunged deep into thought,
    Wondering how it could possibly be,   370
And what was the cause,
That he was so dreaded and feared;
How, when he willed to do good,
With no question or doubt,
Another impulse took over   375
Which thrust that intention aside
And forced him away from the good,
Pushing him fast toward the opposite goal.
That criminal thought
Made him roundly hate God   380
—God our Father in Heaven!—
With a dark scorn learned from the Devil.
He thought that misfortune
Must have come from his birth

And his mother was guilty,   385
Who had never explained what she should:
She surely knew the stain and the taint—
The cause of his sinful behavior.
He raised his eyes toward the heavens,
Summoned thereto by the Holy Ghost,   390
Who let him know, however surprising and odd,
That he yet might become a true friend of God.

N ow Robert swore a solemn oath
     By the nails of the Cross, by the death
And then rebirth of Jesus the Christ,   395
Who shaped and made and created the world,
That he would seek no pleasure or repose
Until he'd have learned
What made him so wicked and evil a man.
Hardly pausing to breathe,   400
He ran upstairs to his mother's chamber,
His sword unsheathed,
Bright and gleaming in the sunlight.
The Duchess drew near
And dropped to the feet of her son,   405
Fearing she was soon bound to die.

"My son," she cried, "what are you doing?
What is the crime, what the offense,
That makes you so ready to slay me?"

Said Robert, "You have to tell me,   410
Or you shall die right away,
Since you can't live any longer
If you don't say, with no moment's delay,
Why I am such an impious creature
And so marked by misfortune   415
That I cannot see a creature of God
And not need to attack him."

"My son," she replied, "God forbid

That I tell you the truth,
For with great pain and great shame   420
You would kill me once you knew;
No mercy for me would stop you."

Robert replied, "Have no fear!
You know the truth;
Tell it to me right away!   425
But if you lie or seek a delay,
I'll make this gleaming sharp sword
Drink the blood in your brain."

His mother, alarmed and afraid,
Recounted, in fear and distress,   430
The truth, the whole tale, of his birth.
She broke the seal; she revealed
God's refusal to heed her unceasing prayers
That he grant her a child.
She turned at that point to the Devil,   435
Who—yes, it was true—was quick to oblige.
He gave her the child she desired
No sooner than she'd asked for his aid.
Thus it was that Robert could do no good,
For God had no part in his being;   440
He stemmed from Hell, where evil dwells,
Running out but to do its villainous work.

"Dear son, no more than that do I know how to say."

Robert, at those words, trembled with wrath.
What his mother, the Duchess, revealed   445
Filled him with sorrow and shame.
He wept tears of pity and shed bitter tears;
Thickly they flowed from his eyes
And streamed down his face,
A face that ever before was unmoved and ice-cold.   450
It was a river of tears.

"Mother," he said, "the time has now come
For a final leave-taking.
Nevermore, if God, the true Martyr, agrees,
Shall the Devil be part of my being!   455
Nevermore, however hard he may try,
Shall he, in whatever way,
Have me again in his service!
I now strip him of the servant I've been!
Now I shall go, with no further delay,   460
To seek out the Pope
And ready myself for harsh penance
For all the crimes and base sins
That have sullied and besmirched my whole being."

He shook his arm and showed a fist;   465
He threw away his sword forthwith;
He called for shears and cut his hair
As closely as he dared.

H is hair cut off,
He leaned against a pillar   470
And pulled off his shoes,
Then quickly ran
To a storeroom close by,
Where he found an old cloak;
He stripped himself bare of his clothes   475
And put on instead just the rough old cloak
Over a sleeveless frock.
He suffered no further delay,
But in tears took leave of his mother,
Who was struck by such grief for her son   480
That she almost lost all her senses.
Thus Robert departed,
A turn to the Lord now ensured in his heart.

Nowhere did he stop along that long road
—No castle or city or town could detain him—   485
Until he arrived at Saint Gilles in Nîmes

And then at Saint James.
From Compostela he continued to Rome,
There to seek confession to the Pope.
But all his efforts, 490
Amid cries and shouts and pushing,
Brought him nowhere near the Pope,
For people had gathered in such numbers,
From places large and small,
To make confession or to voice requests, 495
And the jostling and pushing of the crowd
Before the gate were so great
That no one was admitted
Who'd brought no gift or had no wealth,
So Robert had no chance to speak, 500
Which left him wretched and bewildered.
Cleverly, shrewdly, he inquired,
Since nothing else was possible,
Where and how the Pope would spend his day.
A passerby who knew such things 505
Provided him with all he'd need to know.
Each day at dawn, he said,
A private chapel was prepared
For the holy man of Rome,
The apostolic figure, 510
At Saint John's, his haunt and home,
Where every day he celebrated Mass,
But for no gift or silver present
Might any stranger hear those sacred words.
He was in fact surrounded by assistants, 515
Who sheltered him from all intruders;
No one, for any reason at all,
Saw him before his return from the chapel;
And then it was no one he didn't care to see,
No one he feared might disturb his retreat. 520

When Robert learned this news,
He found his way to the chapel.
After vespers, toward nightfall,

He saw the church grow shadowy and dark.
He saw the beadle lock the door   525
And lantern light then cease to glow.
Robert, ever bold and daring,
Found a little hiding place
Under a handsome stall
Near the chapel altar,   530
Where the Pope was wont to sit.
Pontifical privacy was a prohibition to outwit!

Once the beadle had locked the door
    And made it clear he'd not come back,
It was not until the break of day   535
That the chapel was again prepared
To have the Pope return,
When he would once again sing Mass.
He did indeed appear at dawn,
Along with two old, white-haired priests;   540
He brought no greater entourage,
Apart from doormen who were charged to guard
The doors and to protect all those within.
The holy man had no reason to delay;
He donned his vestments   545
And performed God's sacred rite.
When Mass had ended,
Robert did what Robert had to do.
He bounded from his hiding place
And sprang forward toward the Pope.   550
He flung himself down upon the ground
And threw his arms around one leg
So tightly and so urgently
And held the Pope so painfully
That he could make no move.   555
Robert, risking his life
To save his soul,
Cried out his anguish,
Begging for mercy as he wept.
The doormen came running,   560

One after another,
Hitting and beating and throwing him about,
But through it all
And despite their blows,
He would not unhand his captive,   565
But held the Pope fast and secure.
The doormen would have killed him
And he'd have rendered up his soul,
Had the holy man not shouted protest
And ordered they stand back and let him be.   570
The scoundrels then stepped back,
And left the sinner
Sprawled out at the Pope's two feet.
His life, he said, was cursed;
Woe, he lamented, that he had ever been sired,   575
But more woe that he'd ever been born!

"Friend," said the Pope,
"Who are you, and what's brought about
Such distress as I hear?
Tell me, if you can."   580

"My lord," he replied, "the grievous distress
That I feel is all too quickly revealed.
Of all the world's sinners, I am surely the greatest,
Too selfish and greedy
Ever to heed, ever to love, the heavenly King.   585
My lord, I shall tell you my story.
The duke of the Normans begot me
And the Duchess, his wife, is my mother.
Seventeen years she'd been barren
Before growing pregnant with me   590
However fervently she'd prayed
That it please God to send her a child.
Her prayers long went unanswered.
She felt, in the end, such wrath and despair
That she lost all trust in the Lord,   595
All confidence and hope.

She turned to the Devil to ask for a son,
And the Devil, with his craft, crafted me!
Because it was thus that I came to be,
I undertook such war against our Lord   600
As stripped away my very soul.
My only hope for absolution lies in you;
I see no other way; I know not what to do."

Then he recounted, from beginning to end,
All his crimes and misdeeds,   605
His knavery and wickedness.
One by one, he recounted his sins.
His shame, as he spoke, was too great:
He kept his head low and his eyes filled with tears.
The thought filled him with fear   610
That the Devil might seize his life-weary soul;
That was the fear that made him tremble with cold.

As the Pope listened,
The tale sounded familiar,
For surely he had heard of this case once before.   615
He was perplexed and wondered what he could do.
Robert had done so much that was bad,
Had sinned so greatly and had been so disloyal
That it was hard not to marvel.
It was a grievous task to offer him counsel,   620
And the Pope knew not how to proceed.
Robert, whose face was drenched in tears
That flowed without cease from his heart,
That reddened his eyes and left streaks in his cheeks,
Kept imploring mercy and forgiveness   625
For all the harm he had done in his youth,
When devilish madness drove him on.
The Pope was moved deeply
By such repentance and regret
But didn't know what penance   630
He should order or expect.
He turned at last to Robert and said,

"My friend, this is what you must do:
You shall come with me tonight
But not stay long.   635
In the morning, at the sight of dawn,
I will give you a letter.
You will take the road up to the mountains,
To a forest that is long and broad,
The forest we call Marabonde.   640
Follow that road
And in no time at all,
You'll reach a quiet spring
Half hidden in a valley.
You will follow the stream to the right   645
And then will discover a remarkable site
With a house and a chapel,
Where no one shouts or calls out.
A little hammer hangs at the door,
Oh, very small and light to the touch.   650
You will strike three times and no more
At the door in back, and then sit down.
A little while later, after a pause,
A holy man will come to answer your call,
The good man who dwells in that place.   655
Nowhere in the world lives a holier hermit;
No day goes by in his cabin
Without a miracle performed for him by God;
This often draws a heavy crowd.
Three times a year I seek confession   660
With that saintly man of glory,
So pious, so precious
That many a sinner has been helped by him.
Give him my humble greetings
And hand him my letter.   665
He will not fail to recognize your name,
Since your story will be known to him
Before you exit from his dwelling,
For the letter, when he reads it,
Will tell him all there is to know of you,   670

And he, through God and his grace,
Will quickly know, in the briefest of time,
What penance to prescribe for your sins.
Accept with no qualms his wise discipline."

When Robert had grasped   675
   The reply just voiced
By the holy Pope of Rome
(Known to all as a virtuous man),
He was greatly relieved—indeed, overjoyed;
He wept as he kissed the Pope's two feet.   680
He followed him then
Toward the papal chambers,
Where the Pope himself set down in writing
The letter meant for that saint of a hermit.
When that was done, he affixed his seal.   685
At dawn the next day, he summoned the sinner,
Handed the letter into his care,
And ordered him to leave for the forest
Where the hermit dwelled.
Robert went off—may God guide his steps   690
And may he, in his mercy,
Let him reach a true reunion
With his precious Mother,
Who is radiant with love for him.
And may we, governed likewise and nourished   695
By his law, see ourselves equally flourish!

Robert went off, hastening his steps,
   More eager than ever
To reach our Lord as ably as he could,
By whatever effort, at whatever cost.   700
Arduous travel through woods and forest
Led him at last to the hermitage.
He found the little hammer hanging at the door
And struck his three light blows.
There soon appeared the hermit himself,   705
The holy man, with hair twixt white and gray.

He hobbled forward,
Leaning on a crutch,
His head bent low and covered by a cap of white.
He opened the small door and spoke: 710

"Bless you," he said.

Robert replied that he humbly sought
The hospitality of the old man's house.
The hermit, with great courtesy,
Bade him enter: his guest would have   715
Whatever hospitality was his to offer.
The noble man of highest birth
Bent low to enter through the narrow door.
He voiced the greeting
Of the Pope in Rome   720
And handed his letter to the holy man.
He took little time
To understand the meaning of the message,
For he quickly grasped its purpose.
Once he had read it   725
From beginning to end,
He took his seat and wept tender tears:

"My brother," he said, "how dire the day
When you came to be born!
I see you have come here to seek   730
Penance for the sins
That have blackened your soul.
No man alive, however devoted to God,
Can say what penance is due,
And I am no more able than another.   735
This much, though, will I promise you:
You shall have whatever help is in my power.
Early in the morning, when I behold
The secret of the sacrament, at that salutary time
When the Host, our Lord, lies in my hand,   740
I will humbly pray

That he in all his goodness
Send me a sign
Whereby to recognize your penance;
For God, if he chooses mercy for you,   745
Will instruct me
In the manner of your redemption.
Be now filled with repentance and regret
For all the sins you have committed,
So that tomorrow they may be remitted."   750

Hearing this, Robert sighed in his heart
And felt how utterly contemptible he was;
He wept the tears of a man enraged.
He had lost such weight and grown so pale
That home in Normandy, his native land,   755
He would have passed now for a stranger.
The holy hermit led him to lodgings
And fed him bread and eggs with cool fresh water;
He treated him that night with kind regard,
With all the care Saint Julian would have counseled.   760
He brought him soft green grass to sleep on,
And Robert lay down for a night of rest.
But neither grass nor any other bed
Could bring him that night his desired repose,
For he spent all that time in sore lament   765
For all his sins—and in dreadful fright
Lest he lose our God of Paradise
And the Devil in the end exact his price.

At start of day, when dawn broke through,
The saintly hermit then arose,   770
Took his lantern and candle
And came to waken Robert.
He instructed him to follow to the chapel,
And Robert bounded up to heed his call.
He went with the hermit to worship,   775
To hear how he invoked the Lord.
No sooner, though, was he in that holy place

Than he dropped face down before the altar,
Stretched out in prayer.
Never was there a prisoner in chains   780
Who prayed so mightily to God
To deliver him from Hell
As Robert did with all his heart,
Begging with ardor for pardon and mercy.
He drenched the ground beneath him   785
With tears that flowed
Unceasing down his cheeks.
Please God to grant him
What he so fervently desires!
The holy hermit then endeavored   790
To carry out his service fittingly.
Once he had sung his matins
And recited the hours of prime,
He shed his morning clothes
And quickly donned his proper vestments.   795
Then he began in simple wise
The precious holy Mass
Of God and of the Virgin
Who gave him birth.
The holy man intoned the Mass   800
And, at the moment of the consecration,
When he held the very body of our Lord,
With worshipful heart
And eyes streaming with tears,
He implored the Lord to send him   805
Guidance and counsel
Wherewith to find for Robert a proper penance
Befitting a long and painful repentance.

Just then he saw a hand stretched out
Before him, holding forth for him   810
A tiny message, which he took.
A man of instruction and properly taught,
He perused all the letters contained in the missive,
Reading all the way through, from beginning to end.

The reading left him as overjoyed as he'd have been   815
Embracing the feet of our Lord!
He completed his Mass with no delay,
Then turned to Robert with his news:
The penance that God had in store for him.
The good-hearted hermit   820
Addressed him then with joyful words:

"My friend, now listen to this news:
God wants you to be healed!
You must not be alarmed
By what I shall tell you,   825
Which in a moment you will hear—
But I have a dreadful fear
The penance that God wants of you
May be heavier than you can bear."

"Sir," replied Robert, "bear this in mind: 830
Nothing in the world would I refuse to do
To save my soul from the Devil's grasp;
I refuse to recognize his due!"

The hermit replied, "God loves you,
As his counsel proves.   835
Listen now, my good dear friend,
And you shall hear what you must do
To make God's wish for you come true.

"First of all—and this is God's command—
Your penance must start in this manner: 840
You take on the air of a madman
—Though a simpleton will do—and let
Sword-wielding, stone-throwing rascals
Chase you through the streets.
But wherever you are,   845
Take care that you never strike back.
Make such a show of your madness
That they will all run away,

All those coarse and brutal bullies,
Once they've had their fun with you.   850
Let not a day go by
Without being sure to attract the attention
Of townsmen in great numbers,
Even up to twenty thousand;
They will gladly hoot at you,   855
Throw stones and push and call you fool.

"This penance, my friend, is only the first;
It is fearsome and cruel—
But the penance that follows is harsher,
More bitter still, and more painful.   860
Once you have left this place, take care,
Wherever you are,
That you not speak, whatever you see,
But always remain perfectly mute.
Should any word escape from your lips,   865
Be the need wise, be the need foolish,
Back you will go to serving the Devil.
That is the truth, not a fable or lie.
Still, I may give you permission to speak
And then you may certainly do so;   870
Only then, with no sin or misconduct,
May you give voice to your tale;
Be silent till then, and your penance can't fail.

"Robert, dear friend, listen now
To the third command, brutal and bitter,   875
Which will leave you haggard, with matted hair.
Listen now to God's command:
Take care to eat no food,
However much your hunger drives you
Or whatever longing you may feel,   880
Unless it be food you have wrested from dogs;
Other food would not feed your soul
Or help you toward salvation.
My friend, now you have heard

All three of the Lord's commands."   885

The joy Robert felt was intense;
He said he would heed every command
And not one would he overlook or forget,
Even were he to live a thousand years.
The hermit consulted his message again   890
And saw one final point
To be brought to Robert's attention.

"Dear friend," said the priest,
"I see one further thing you should know.
If ever a man should approach you,   895
Whoever he may be, a man of any sort,
Who bids you in the name of God
To carry out some task, do it—
Provided he can show good faith by spelling out
The three extraordinary penances   900
That in God's name I have imposed on you.
Now be brave, be sensible and prudent.
Knowing now the whole great task
That our Lord has deigned to assign you,
Prostrate yourself upon this ground   905
And ask his mercy as you lie face down."

Robert lay prostrate, face down,
Utterly and wholly in the hands of our Lord,
Determined that the Devil not seize him.
The hermit, before he rose from the floor,   910
Absolved him of his sins,
So that never again would they sully his soul
And that the Devil would disclaim him for good.
Then Robert went off on his own,
Starting out for the city of Rome.   915

He came to Rome early one morning,
A heavy staff in his hand.
No sooner had he passed through the gate

Than he started to strike and jostle and bray,
So that townsmen came out 920
To see what was wrong.
Robert saw no one appear
Whom he didn't attempt to attack:
He was known through town in no time at all.
The Romans all thought him thoroughly mad 925
And came out in droves to attack in return.
The more he advanced, the louder their howls—
With mud and with muck, with dung and with dirt,
With rags and old shoes,
With lungs of sick cows and filthy soiled mats, 930
They rushed him, they beat him and struck him;
They had game there to feast on.
Robert, meanwhile, who could hardly stand still,
Kept twisting and turning,
Pretending to strike back and kill; 935
Thus he chased them around
In every direction,
Though it was only a feint on his part.
Now were they all truly convinced
He was too mad to have any regard 940
For all the harm they might inflict on him.
Brutes and crude thugs, they all
Wounded and injured him badly;
No stone or rock did they find too hard or too sharp
Wherewith to pelt him close to his heart. 945
The moment then came when Robert
Could endure no more of these blows
That left him defenseless,
For the ruffians and brutes
Had beaten him so 950
That his flesh was torn and was bleeding.
Could he have stayed any longer
Amidst all of those people
Coming from one side and another
To stone him and shout for his death? 955
Fear made his flesh go wet with sweat.

No longer was the pain to be borne;
Strength ebbed away and so did his breath.
He set out to flee without looking back,
Heading straight up the hill to the tower   960
That stood high in the heart of the city.
There he saw the olden palace,
Where the Emperor then lived.
You have never yet heard such a story
As now you will hear from me;   965
But close your eyes, the better to see!

The Emperor in question
    Was the best endowed in all the world
With courtliness and prowess,
With valor and largess.   970
He was stuck, however, at a sorry pass,
For every day he faced attacks
By a seneschal of his, whose feats of war
Had brazenly and wrongfully
Brought devastation to his land.   975
Here, I can tell you, is how it all began:
The Emperor had a daughter
So beautiful that no one knew
Of any maiden in the world as beautiful as she.
But some deed unknown,   980
Disloyal and sinful, no doubt not of her own,
Had left the girl unfit to speak and utterly mute.
She understood whatever was said,
Whatever she heard, whether foolish or wise,
But from her lips no word ever issued   985
And her thoughts were conveyed just by signs.
Thanks to the damsel's remarkable beauty
And ineffable charm,
The seneschal fell deeply in love.
For his love he'd have gone stripped and unshod   990
To the end of the world,
If only he had his golden-haired love.
He asked her hand of the Emperor

And would have been thrilled
To take her home as his wife. 995
But her father, the Emperor, so clung to his child
That an instant sufficed to dismiss the man's suit
With an outright, offensive denial.
The maiden, he said, was his only successor
And too young, besides, to be anyone's bride; 1000
No—he rejected the seneschal's suit.
When the man was denied the maiden he loved,
He was deeply distressed and fiercely offended,
For his rank could hardly be nobler
And his wealth was immense, 1005
With twenty towns and thirty castles
And four Lombardian cities;
In many a year no braver man
Had anyone seen than he;
No more powerful lord was master of so much 1010
Or held vaster domains.
He went to war against the Emperor
For so flatly rejecting his suit.
He laid waste to his land and ravaged his towns;
He plundered his way right up to Rome; 1015
Nowhere did anyone stand in his way
To a field, to a road, to a meadow.
His knightly success
Let him lay siege to the city.
No man therein had courage enough 1020
To venture far from his door.
The Emperor's great army
Was dispersed and disbanded,
And the siege left the Emperor with nowhere to go;
His fear of the foe was uncommonly great, 1025
But the Lombardy road gave him no way to escape.

Thus the state of things was dire
At the time when Robert arrived in the city.
Mad though he seemed, well out of his mind,
He found his way up to the palace. 1030

There the Emperor was seated,
Eating his meal at the high table,
When Robert ran in, heading straight for him,
But the head of the staff,
Weapon in hand, tried to bar him the way.   1035
Robert, who dared not stand still
With servants beating and thrashing his back
And pushing him away toward a different room,
Boldly and with all the strength he had left
Dashed past the guards on the porch   1040
And dropped, gasping and panting,
At the feet of the Emperor.
There he stopped and stayed still;
A long moment went by as he remained without moving.
The guards came in running   1045
And with thick sticks in their hands
Dealt him blows meant to harm and to cripple;
No attempt, though, did he make to stand up;
And no matter how hard they struck him and hit,
To their will he would never submit.   1050

W hen the Emperor realized
     That his guards had their hands on a madman,
He cried out in a thunderous voice
That no one should strike him or hurt him
And that he would be the madman's protector.   1055
He approached the man most likely to help:

"Let him be given something to eat!"

The Emperor's command was immediately followed,
So Robert was given white bread
And a full goblet of wine,   1060
Along with a bowl filled with meat.
All this was he served on a mat
Of freshest green grass.
But what a stunning, perplexing response,
For Robert dashed it all brusquely aside   1065

With a distaste he felt no reason to hide!

T he Emperor exclaimed, "He's brushed it aside!
       He has lost his wits to such an extent
That madness alone suffices to feed him."

Then he asked all to let the man be   1070
Until he felt hungry and remembered to eat.
Robert was then for the time left alone,
While no one attempted to touch him
Or even to speak;
Nor did he breathe a word to anyone else.   1075
Everyone present was intent just on dinner.
The Emperor, formal as ever,
Had his place, eating and drinking,
At the head of the table.
To lighten his meal,   1080
He was served the bone of a stag,
With sinews still dangling.
He drew out the marrow,
Consumed it with pleasure
And, once he had eaten his fill,   1085
Let the bone drop to the floor.
Under the table lay a bloodhound
Twenty years old if a day;
Since he had been so effective a hunter,
Better by far than all other dogs,   1090
The Emperor remained so fondly attached
That he was allowed to scrounge as he wished
Under the table and all through the room,
Never hearing a word of reproach.
The dog saw the bone fall to the floor   1095
—A treat he could hardly have spurned!—
He ran to retrieve it; his teeth greedily seized it;
But little time did he have to savor his prize,
As Robert ran up beside him
And tore the bone from his grip.   1100
Robert chewed and he gnawed;

So powerfully pressed by his hunger,
No way would he ever let go.
Now at last he had something to eat!
He gnawed and he slurped with rapacious delight.   1105
The Emperor let out a laugh and exclaimed,

"What a remarkable sight!
I've never seen anything like it.
This fool, who wasted his time without eating
And rejected good food,   1110
Now wrests a dry meatless bone
From the dog's very jaw
And chews it with ravenous joy!
Truly out of his mind, and it shows!"

Then once again he told his good servants,   1115
Ever ready to please him,
To bring in large helpings of food,
More than enough to satisfy the fool,
Who was clearly beset by ravening hunger.
But Robert would approach no relief of the sort,   1120
Unless he could tear it from the teeth of the dog.
With no delay, the servants brought in
Bread and meat in heaping abundance.
Robert would now have his stomach's desire!
He greeted the Emperor's command   1125
With a joy they could all understand.

At the Emperor's command,
His hunters came forward
To feed his old hound good wholesome bread,
Not a treat to refuse!   1130
No sooner, however, was it in the dog's mouth
Than Robert sprang forth in one bound
And snatched the bread for himself;
No other approach would have led him to touch it,
But now he bore down with visible pleasure.   1135
A joiner would not have been so eager

To devour his meal, nor a peasant
Coming home hungry from the field,
As was Robert bolting down chunks of his bread.
The Emperor and others around him   1140
Found this all very funny
And everyone laughed and declared
They had never yet seen so fantastic a fool,
A madman too amusing to muzzle.
The hunters tossed meat to the dog   1145
And meant no offense as they did so;
He'd have caught it and eaten with pleasure,
If only he had had a real chance,
But Robert snapped it up with his teeth
And bit off his part along with the bread.   1150
He looked so fierce as he seized it
And devoured the bread and the meat so intently
That no one could watch such excitement
And not break into loud peals of laughter.
The Emperor, enjoying the scene,   1155
Swore by his beard and his head:
Harm to the madman would be harm to oneself!
For as long as he stayed in this court,
Woe, lest anyone touch him!
Not for a hundred gold marks   1160
Would he wish the madman away;
If he could stay at his court,
They should let him move about freely,
With no constraint or restraint,
Inside the palace or even outside,   1165
For the man was a fool, but untouched by guile.

When Robert had eaten enough
And his hunger had passed,
He took crusts and large pieces of bread,
Stuffed all those morsels into his mouth,   1170
Then crawled on all fours toward the dog,
The nicest, gentlest hound that ever was,
And offered the bread in his mouth

To the mouth of the dog,
Who took it and ate.   1175
By the end of such feeding and more,
The dog was more pleased, with a belly more full,
Than had ever been true
In all his years in the palace.
This day he was grateful and glad,   1180
For Robert had come to befriend him.
When he was full, he went right off to rest
Under the stairs where he would normally lie.
Robert went after, overcome as he was
By a need for repose and for sleep.   1185
Had he not spent a day
Taking blows and harsh beatings
And feeling the pain of his multiple wounds?
Robert lay down alongside the hound.
They lay there under a vault   1190
Of the Emperor's chapel,
A magnificent spot, a retreat like no other.
Robert could rejoice with good reason,
For now every day from this place
He might hear, as he wished,   1195
Two masses or three, perhaps even four.
The Emperor decided to see him
And sat down to watch
Whatever he'd do,
But Robert, the good-natured fool,   1200
Went back to sleep right away.
The Emperor had no wish to disturb him,
So left him to sleep in peace
And returned to the palace,
Where he ordered that no one trouble his fool.   1205
He commanded his men
To place fodder and hay and good straw
With the dogs under the vault;
That's where he wanted a bed for the madman
And, if his neck were to hurt,   1210
A soft pillow to cradle his head.

This was all done just as he said.

R obert now had no cause for complaint,
  Since his bed was the one that he wanted
And he had a protector who without any prompting   1215
Made sure he was fed
Just as the hermit had ordered.
Now he could lie down to rest
Or stand up to stretch however he wished.
When he had had enough sleep,   1220
He made the sign of the cross and stood up on his feet;
He was thirsty and parched and, needing relief,
He went out in search of fresh water.
To find his way through the palace,
He wandered one way and another,   1225
Coming at last to a flourishing garden,
A spot of great beauty where no one was present.
It was planted with trees of all sorts,
With green medicinal herbs and good roots
Such as were used to prepare elixirs and cures.   1230

O rchard and garden, it surrounded a fountain
  So sparkling and clear, so gentle and pure
That he had never before seen one so lovely.
Its water flowed through the chamber
Of the Emperor's dear daughter,   1235
Its surface as smooth as a mirror.
The noble young lady
Had had a window created
High above the garden to the right.
The window was exceedingly narrow,   1240
With room for no one but her
To sit there and enjoy the sight of the trees.
The maiden, in the first blush of girlhood,
Often went to the window
To pass the time with calm pleasure;   1245
From there she could hear the murmuring sea
And cast her glance across the fields;

The place was enchantingly wholesome and fresh.

Now let's turn back to the garden and Robert.
He went straight to the fountain,   1250
Which stood by itself in the center;
He slaked his thirst with generous draughts
And, when he had drunk all the water he wished,
He went back to lie down under the vault.
He slept with the dogs in their litter of straw   1255
Till the song of the quail awoke him at dawn.

At the first sight of light, at the breaking of dawn,
The good Emperor woke and arose
To hear Mass, as he normally did.
The noble, stout-hearted lord   1260
First in his chapel listened to matins
And then, in the day's early calm,
Heard the solemn high Mass.
Robert, grateful,
There where he lay under the stairs,   1265
There where he lay just as he wished,
Quietly wept as he thought of his sins,
As his heart cried to God;
And to merit redemption
With his whole being he prayed   1270
For the mercy and love of the Lord;
This was the constant concern of his soul.
Following Mass, and for long,
He softly bemoaned his many past sins;
Then, after much weeping,   1275
Beseeching and praying,
He dashed out through the main streets of Rome.

He ran and he pranced like a man out of his mind,
He skipped and he hopped,
Braying and bleating, snorting and snuffling,   1280
Hardly disposed to hide from the crowd.
Boys and young men,

Children as well, ran behind him,
But it was not just to watch or only to jeer:
They punched him and kicked him,   1285
Knocked him down and beat him up.
When they had so pummeled
And pounded and trounced him
That he could no longer take all that torment,
He breathlessly found his way back   1290
To the stairs, his refuge from harm.
There he waited and watched
In peace, without trouble or danger,
Until it was time for the Emperor's repast.
When he saw that the moment was right   1295
And he felt quite sure
That the first course had been served,
He went to sit down with no further delay
In the place where the hound was ready and waiting.
No doorman stood in his way   1300
To stop him from moving about as he pleased.
A place was already set for his presence,
And Robert had no need of a napkin!
The Emperor had charged one of his men
To look after Robert and give him his food.   1305
The man tended only to him
And did so with pleasure;
He threw food to the dog and then watched
Robert rush forward to seize it with such strength
As the hound had no power to match;   1310
Then he chewed and he ate with hungry delight.
The Emperor was vastly amused
And so were all others who were there for the feast;
It was funny to see the fool besting the beast.

S hould anyone try to detail   1315
   The unending follies
That Robert found himself led to,
I do think he'd have too much to recount.
What a bore it would be to go over it all!

Indeed, there is nothing really to add   1320
At this point in the story—
Better to stop here for a while!
But this much I can tell you in truth:
That Robert went on for ten years
With his struggle, with help from the Emperor.   1325
He ventured out every day,
Walking through Rome with heart-stopping fear,
Paying the price of his torturous penance,
And then, at the end of this daily trial,
He'd lie down with the hound   1330
Under his high vaulted cover.
The dog knew him too well
Ever to part from his side,
Following Robert
Wherever he went.   1335
And if he was the first to receive
A morsel of food, he came up to Robert
Clenching it tightly,
Just as he'd learned,
Then left it for Robert to take;   1340
And once he had taken his part,
The dog, at long last, had his meal.
Day after day, without fail,
This was how Robert performed his long penance,
And all in such silence   1345
That no one could know what he was doing.
Not a thing was revealed,
For to no one did he utter his secret;
Never in the fullness of ten long years,
For any reason whatever,   1350
Did a word good or ill, wise or foolish,
Pass his closed lips.
Everyone thought, without any doubt,
That he'd been mute since his birth;
Nor could anyone learn the name that he bore   1355
Or discern whence he came
Or even his land and his language.

Everyone thought him a dimwit and fool.
Had there been a brother or sister to see him
In the state he was in, 1360
They would never have known him.
He was so changed by his ills and his sins
And so deeply committed to penance
That he never allowed, in ten long years,
Any infraction of rules he had sworn to. 1365
The Emperor, for his part, took good care of his fool,
For he found pleasure in his antics
And relief from troubled thoughts;
The fool made him laugh and gave him good cheer.
He kept him dressed every day 1370
In a fine hooded cloak
That went down past his knees.
The people of Rome all recognized Robert—
Women and clergy and laymen,
Ladies and damsels, 1375
Maidservants in their chambers,
And, need I add, the Emperor's daughter.
For all, I can tell you, for great and for small,
Robert became their preferred entertainer;
He was laughter itself; 1380
They marveled at the fun their jester provided;
They themselves learned
To ape his dumb capers
And follow his lead, however inane.

Now I can add—and it's not out of line— 1385
What kind of life and what pleasure
Robert's role as a penitent allowed him to lead.
Through ten years of penance,
He let not a single day pass
Without the delight of spending a moment 1390
At the spring in the garden
Under the window of the Emperor's young daughter.
Every day, she watched him come and take a long drink
And then go on his way.

With that, I have told you all I could say   1395
Of Robert's life throughout those long days.

I n the course of the time that I'm telling about,
A surge of overweening pride so stirred the seneschal
Who held the land around
That he took up arms and went to war   1400
Against his rightful lord, the Emperor.
Rome was gripped by such dark terror
That it would have gladly paid for peace
If only the invader consented to withdraw.
The seneschal, though, swore by God   1405
And the Cross, indeed the very sepulchre
Where our Savior lay entombed,
That peace would never come to Rome
Unless the Emperor granted him his daughter
And the crown that came along with her.   1410
The Emperor, generous of heart,
But just as firmly resolute,
Responded that the day would never come
When he'd give up his noble daughter,
So beautiful and svelte, so bright and wise;   1415
He would rather let himself be hanged upon a tree,
Be drowned in waters at the shore,
Or lose his head to a traitor's sword.

W hat now shall I add to the story?
The war was bitter and harsh,   1420
With no pause by the man in love with his love.
The Romans, I can tell you,
Had little defense in the face of his forces;
All they could do was endure the assault,
Double their archers and strengthen their walls,   1425
Which again and again they had to repair.
News of the fight flew far from the field,
So no country was left in the world
Without talk and reports of the war
(And the news of the Emperor's troubles),   1430

No place where the word had not yet been heard
That Rome was no more a center of joy
But was now so deeply distressed,
So disturbed and dejected
That the Romans were prisoners in their city,   1435
With a garrison reduced by two thirds.
It was said that they had but two years to live.
These tidings were swift to come to the ears
Of the Turks in Asia Minor.
From Khorasan in Persia, from the Caspian coast,   1440
Princes and kings assembled;
With arrogance and pride and ambition
They gathered their armies and met.
With whispered plans and muttered words
They recognized their chance to march on Rome: 1445
The men and women in the city
Were weak, despondent, in distress.
The place that once had dispossessed the Turks
Would now again be theirs to rule!
They laced pennants to their lances   1450
And refurbished all their arms.
So well did they conceal their moves
That Rome had no hint of their cunning
Before their few scouts come home running.

The Turks readied their move with no delay,   1455
  Equipping their ships and loading the boats.
Once they'd fully prepared,
They resolved not to tarry in port,
But set sail pushed by favoring winds
And with hearts boldly ready   1460
To capture and ravage the city of Rome.
Oh, how I wish they'd have perished first,
Before trying to bring such destruction to Rome
And force the good Emperor from his throne!
The Turks sailed off, the winds obliging,   1465
The yards unfurled against the masts,
The sailors eager and expectant.

They swept ahead and traveled fast
Till they reached the port of the city,
Where the evildoers banked their ships   1470
And poured men and their arms onto the shore.
They set up tents and large pavilions;
Their camp stretched far along the beach,
Two leagues at least, and ready for battle.
Their shields and helmets and banners,   1475
Gonfalons and standards and thousands of arms
Glistened and flashed their threat in the sun.
The foes that sought an end to Rome
Were too soon massed at every gate and door,
So nothing now could stave off a war.   1480

The Turks rode down through the plains,
   Plundering and stealing, killing the peasants,
Setting houses ablaze and smashing the churches,
Rooting out gardens and cutting down trees.
Oh, Rome had good cause to lament!   1485
The hue and the cry, the clamor and din,
The panic and shouting—it all reached
The ramparts of Rome and plunged
The people who dwelled in the city
Into turmoil and anguish and terror.   1490
What onslaught did they face—what lay in store?
Romans rose from every side,
Climbed on high to gaze across the plain,
Raced up the towers as high as they could.
They saw the countryside ablaze   1495
As it had never been before,
Torched this time by flames of war.
And with it all, they saw fields covered
With heavy helmets and with countless spears
That bespoke a foe as yet unknown.   1500
Upon the sea they could discern a host
That in no time at all
Had spread along the full length of the beach.
They realized then, without a doubt,

That this was not a seneschal   1505
Taking up arms to win a lady!
Even calm, cool-headed men were frightened.
In the midst of it all, a messenger
Came running through the streets,
Where throngs were dashing here and there   1510
In all directions through the city,
Trembling and crying and weeping with fear.

"Woe," he cried, "you blind and foolish people!
You don't see what you're facing!
These are Turks from Anatolia,   1515
Persian Khorasan, and the Caspian coast;
That's who's arrived at our Roman port!
Ready yourselves for battle! Everyone's dead,
Unless you can mount a forceful defense
And meet them in a furious fight;   1520
For once they've laid siege to the city,
Everyone here will be trapped without exit or pity."

When the Romans heard the messenger
Deliver so appalling a message,
They felt such terrible fright   1525
That all were moved, even eager,
To risk flight into the pitch-black night.
Ah, God! The dire events
That lay in store for Rome's good Emperor!
His life became a sorry lot,   1530
When news arrived that Turks
Would soon assault the walls.
It grieved him sorely, made him wonder what to do.
He called his senators together,
As well as others entrusted with the law,   1535
And sought the session's useful counsel.
Some urged that he emerge outdoors
To engage the Turks in combat hand to hand:

"God, who has wrought so many wonders

For the welfare of his people,   1540
Would in this battle never leave their side;
We should rely on help unfailingly divine!"

Others present at this session
Expressed a different view: No battle, please!
To fight against the Turks, they were   1545
Far from having all the men they'd need,
Men ready for defense, vigorous and bold.
Still, if anyone could draw
Supportive troops from Lombardy
And persuade the seneschal   1550
To make peace and take command of them
And help campaign against the Turks,
Then have no doubt:
They would together force them out!

This was the plan that by all was accepted,   1555
    By rich men and poor, by young men and old.
They selected as envoys to the seneschal
Two barons he was known to value as friends;
The Emperor accepted their choice
And sent the two men on their mission.   1560
They went where they knew the seneschal to be,
Went as quickly as travel allowed.
They came to his palace to see him
And explained what it was that they needed;
They told him all, held nothing back,   1565
The reasons for their critical mission—
How the Emperor was seeking his help
And how fearful the Romans now felt,
With Turks at the gates, all ready to strike.

"They don't dare to move against them   1570
In any hand-to-hand attack,
So weak is their position
Unless they have your backing and your aid."

The seneschal made no more attempt to listen,
But had his holy relics carried into view   1575
To disconcert the Romans
And fill the Emperor
With such fear and such foreboding
That he would cede him his daughter
Before expecting him to rush to arms.   1580
He swore before the barons,
And asserted with absolute assurance,
Upon the relics that lay before him,
Just as the circumstance required,
That he would rather act to harm the Emperor   1585
And bring devastation to his land
Than aid him in the slightest way . . .
Unless he granted him his daughter
And gave him leave to lie with her in bed.
This was the arrogant, defiant response   1590
That he sent back to the Emperor, his lord.
Now felt the Emperor a deeper pain
Than he could have ever imagined.
He had never been so overwhelmed,
So sorely tried as now he was.   1595
Anguished and anxious, deeply upset,
He everywhere sent word to whatever men
He had reason to command,
But very few responded to his call.
His Holiness, the Pope, however, there in Rome,   1600
Lent him his support.
Noble lords were summoned,
Men of the highest rank,
Senators and barons,
Who all debated the steps to take.   1605
The wisest men among them moved not to delay
A fight against the Turks, should that foe
Show any move to storm the city's walls:
Till then they should defend themselves
Outside, in open country,   1610
And not give the enemy a chance

To fence them in with sword and lance.

T he Emperor accepted the council's advice
   As did the Pope, our Holy Father,
Who exhorted all men to keep watch   1615
And confess and prepare
To do battle with resolve and assurance.
He gave them strength and commitment
With the sermons he pronounced
And his words of encouragement and cheer.   1620
He commanded all people to fast,
Insisting they take a meal
No more than once in a day,
So God might act in their defense
Against the cursèd Turks   1625
Now camped along their shore.
The news now flew through the city;
Ladies and maidens
Wept and cried and lamented,
Stirred by the fear that they felt   1630
For their lovers and brothers,
For their fathers and cousins,
All making ready to move into battle
Against the fell Turkish host.
In the Emperor's apartment   1635
There was such trepidation
That no music was heard, whether played or just sung.
Robert, at home under the stairs,
Felt greater grief and more wrath
Than I can put into words   1640
For the good Emperor, the noble,
Whom he saw so deeply afflicted
Among those of his household.
The Turkish host arrived by sea,
Reaching very close to the city.   1645
They were people with no love for God,
Nonbelievers and faithless all!
Let us now turn to the good, faithful penitent

Who seven full years
Had spent living in Rome;   1650
I'll tell you soon what victory he won,
Once the proper time has come.

One Tuesday morning at break of day
The Turks prepared their army
To lay siege to the walls of the city—   1655
Not, I must say, an easy endeavor!
They arranged all their men in several large groups.
First in line rode the greatest battalions,
The smartest fighters and most stalwart—
A good hundred thousand men,   1660
It's said by those who know such figures.
From Rome they could be seen advancing,
And those in the city trembled with fear.
At the Emperor's order,
Men ran through the streets, taking up arms,   1665
But a mere twenty thousand, no more,
Had the training to fight in real combat.
Ah, God! If only they'd known Robert downstairs,
How quickly they'd have had him
Covered in mail   1670
And led out to face the battalions
Of the fast-approaching Saracens!
But this was not the proper time.
The Emperor made ready in the courtyard
Of his magnificent palace,   1675
Summoning all his troops
To form them into units for combat,
Groups that he wanted to move wisely and well
When facing the Turks,
Who stood at the gates, all ready to surge.   1680

Once he had, standing before him,
Both rich men and poor,
All equipped as if ready for combat,
Prepared to prevail over proud Turkish troops,

He organized his divisions of knights,   1685
Setting up ten battalions
Of two thousand men each.
One he passed on to the Pope,
Unfailingly faithful and loyal,
To act as guardian of the royal dragon banner   1690
And shield it from the nefarious foe.
Standing before his good Romans,
The Emperor ordered, with tears in his eyes,
That they make no further delay:
They must now issue forth against the invaders,   1695
Who were perilously closing in.
His men obeyed without objection.
Apprehensive and filled with misgivings,
They moved to the fields beyond the walls,
The various corps tightly aligned.   1700
With tears in his eyes, the Emperor bade adieu
To his beautiful daughter,
His rose among roses
And dearer to him than all else in his life.
He commended to God the young girls,   1705
The ladies and maidens,
All weeping for him, for love of their lord,
And crying loudly to God
That he preserve him and see to his safety,
So that harm not befall him.   1710

When Robert saw the Roman troops depart,
Tears welled up in his eyes
And started down his cheeks.
Ah, God! How pained he was
To see the Emperor going off alone!   1715
Happily would he have followed him
If it were no transgression of his penance!
That, indeed, was all he feared.
Under the stairs, he couldn't stop weeping;
All by himself, he gave way to his sorrow,   1720
But only in thought—not a word did he utter.

He looked up to our Lord
And silently spoke his address.
Hear now what Robert in his head said:

"Ah, God!" he said in his thoughts,   1725
"You who through spiritual force
Have saved so many a soul
From the people and works of the Devil,
I would gladly run to the aid of the Emperor
And attack those arrogant Turks,   1730
Who are all too puffed up with pride!
I would deal with them so handily
They'd soon be slain
And gone forever from Rome.
But God does not desire   1735
That I stand by his side in this fight.
Indeed, if he deigned to desire my presence,
The Saracens today
Would be crushed as I entered,
For I would be wielding my naked blade,   1740
A strong, tough sword—and swift!
Not for all the gold in Italy
And even if they numbered countless thousands,
Would I not leave them shorn of all powers!"

With that, he stood up straight and sighed   1745
And walked in tears into the garden;
He stayed for a moment at the edge of the spring,
Whose water was clear and sweet to drink,
Then sat down off to a side,
Having no wish to be seen   1750
Overcome with distress and helplessly weeping.
He could think of nothing but God,
Whom in his heart's silence he worshipped,
And prayed that he protect
His Emperor in the imminent battle   1755
Where he too would have wished to be,
Had it pleased the Lord to show him his place—

Had our Lord wished to grant him that grace.

The beautiful maiden
I have mentioned before   1760
Had just come to the fountain and sat in the shade,
Where she meant to avoid any encounter.
She sat by herself, glanced around at one moment,
And noticed Robert, sitting not far.
She saw him at prayer, his hands outstretched   1765
To speak of grace to the Lord.
She sat there in astonishment
And had to wonder how such prayer could be;
It seemed to her that, for all his mad behavior,
No man was mad who could pray like this.   1770
The lovely, gentle maiden
Gave Robert intense and close attention;
She thought him a man worthy of love.
Then she looked out toward the sea
And saw the Turks prepared to attack   1775
And destroy the glory of Rome.
She saw the Romans move against them,
Who had already come so close
That the archers, first in line,
Were battling one another   1780
With crisscrossing arrow volleys,
And many were already dead or injured.

As the maiden stood watching
The clash of those out in front,
There suddenly sprang up at the spring,   1785
At the very spot where Robert was weeping,
A radiantly handsome, noble knight.
His hauberk shone brighter than silver;
His arms and his shield,
Like the straps at his belt,   1790
Were more white than a lily;
He was a ravishing sight to behold.
He wore a broad sword at his hip,

Whose blade gleamed as brightly
As snow freshly fallen from clouds high above,   1795
And the horse he bestrode
Was whiter than the petals of new blossoms;
The white robe that he wore
Endowed his appearance with still greater beauty.
He quickly dismounted before Robert's eyes;   1800
In a moment he spoke—a moment sufficed
For this word from Jesus the Christ:

"Robert, my friend, it is God's command,
    Sent to you here in my voice,
That you enter the battle!   1805
Do not think this to be a mistake,
And if you don't credit my message,
This fact will show you its truth:
I offer as proof
That in a forest surrounded by mountains,   1810
You went in quest of penitence
To the holiest man on earth;
He enjoined so strict a penance
That even one part is a grievous sentence."

When Robert heard this message,   1815
    He felt such wondrous joy
His heart quivered with anticipation.
He turned to the east, his arms outstretched,
To render thanks to his Creator.
He took the envoy's arms and all equipment   1820
And prepared himself for combat.
The maiden was startled
To see him in armor;
Tears appeared in her beautiful eyes,
So deeply moved was she.   1825
Oh! He took pains with his arms,
This Robert who'd soon be a threat to the foe!
He attached his sword and laced on his helmet,
Then sprang in full armor onto his steed

Without any thought to his stirrups.   1830
Once he was armed, he took up his shield
Like the expert he was in the matter,
Trained and skilled in the bearing of arms;
He held his shield by the straps
And seized hold of his heavy, stiff lance.   1835
By the end of the day,
Those arms would make hash of the pagans!
Then he took leave of God's radiant envoy,
Who gave him his blessing.
I think there has never been seen   1840
A knight more richly armed or impressive,
For the protective shield that he had at his neck
Fitted him so well
It seemed a part of his very body.
He took off at a gallop;   1845
No man of any sort has ever seen
A knight depart in such a burst of speed.
Ah, God! If he now had a foe to fight,
What a rough assault there'd be!
The Emperor would soon discover   1850
What man he had fed and protected.
The maiden looked at him
And thought that never in her life
Had she seen a man of no account
Who bore his arms so brilliantly.   1855
But oh, how well she would have understood
Had she but known
The prowess for which now he atoned!

R obert rode off with no delay.
   Rushing ahead without pause   1860
Right past the break in the garden wall
That the peasants had made
To arrive at the fields lying beyond.
Robert then, silent as ever,
Broke past the breach   1865
To reach the plain where the fighting took place.

He went where he heard
The shouting, the noise, and the tumult
Produced by the Saracen forces
With their horns and their trumpets   1870
And drums, which they were sounding
To stun and upset all the horses.
It was a tempest of blasting and blaring!
Robert paused nowhere
Before reaching the Romans;   1875
Nor did he stop at the first that he saw,
But dashed past the many battalions,
The last no less than the first.
They all watched as he passed
And agreed that nowhere had they seen,   1880
Or ever before, so valiant a knight as he.
But when it turned clear
He belonged to no regular troop,
Their surprise even grew.
The Emperor watched in wonder,   1885
Who had moved to the vanguard
To witness the clash of the armies,
For now they were truly
So close to each other
That the hearts of all cowards were trembling.   1890
Robert rode right past the Emperor
Into what he saw was a thick mass
Of Turks and the heaviest fighting.
A sparrow hawk swooping down on a quail
Does not descend with greater dispatch   1895
Than Robert swept down in his dash
Onto Saracen forces.
There where he saw them massed at their thickest,
He struck them so hard that no one was spared:
He toppled one man to the ground   1900
And then threw two of them onto their backs;
Good luck then let him knock down three more.
From his very first charge,
Robert's fierce pride made its mark on the field.

He threaded his way through the Turks   1905
And encountered no man, young or old,
Whom he failed to face down in a trice;
In a very short while, he slew thirty
Who would never again stand up
To the Romans or do harm to their side.   1910
He struck at the Turks with no respite.
Wherever he saw a thick swarm,
He charged and scattered them freely.
The Turks were so cowed and in awe
They didn't dare to await the bite of his lance;   1915
Whenever he started to retrace his steps,
Even the bravest moved out of his way.
The Saracens in no time at all
Were overawed and so daunted by him
That none of them dared to come near,   1920
But no way did they have to avoid
Being caught by Robert's relentless pursuit,
Since his horse was so swift
There was none in the host to compare.
He twisted in and out, this way and that,   1925
Leaving so many men bloodied and spent!
The Turks, though, fought back with their maces,
And what a wonder it was how their blows
Failed time and again to topple their target;
They couldn't stop him, couldn't stun him: 1930
Tougher was he than the best hammered bronze!
In a short time, that first wave of fighters
Was so overwhelmed, they fled from the field
And Robert prepared once more to succeed.

The Emperor, at the head of his army,   1935
    Saw the splendid feats of knighthood
That Robert accomplished in front of his eyes;
He was excited to have such a prize.

He called to his men, "Forward, gallop ahead!
Take care that no one take fright!   1940

The Turks are all as good now as dead,
Their strongest men already defeated,
And the man who slew them is right out in front.
See how he's chasing some off the field
And striking down those who remain! 1945
God! Who is this man of invincible prowess?
Never have I seen, even in dreams,
A man so helpful to us
Or so valorous as he.
Take care there be no man so mean 1950
As to fail to follow his lead!"

No one then failed to gallop ahead
As all lances were courageously lowered.
Now, though, the Turks made a dash for the spot
Where Robert had just shown such bravura. 1955
He had broken his lance
In the body of Khorasan's king.
For never were Apollo or Diana,
Mohammed, or whatever strong god they had,
Empowered to protect them from death. 1960
Robert, who had created this martyr,
Angrily unsheathed his sword
And in he plunged to the pagan throng;
Many a head fell to his weapon.
The Turks fled to escape him, 1965
But the Romans followed Robert
And rushed forward in forceful pursuit—
Though they would have had little success,
Had the foe not been panicked by Robert,
Who had caused them their rout. 1970
He slew; he knocked down; he thrust over;
He killed all the flesh he could gore
With his sharp, flashing sword.

"Like him!" cried the Emperor. "No rest or repose!
That man is a model of courage and prowess, 1975
Ready to slay all our foes!"

The war cry then sounded and swelled,
    As Robert struck one Turk and another,
And put the entire first squadron to flight
By giving them such terrible chase   1980
That no man or woman could have wanted to watch,
Right up to the guard in the rear,
Where the biggest battalion stood waiting.
Those taking flight now fell upon the others,
Bringing panic and disorder into their ranks;   1985
They knew not where to look, where to go.
Robert was so close on their tail,
So eager to lash out and to kill
That not one could stay standing in place.
Even the most daring didn't dare turn   1990
To face him—no, indeed!—
For they dreaded the death of a martyr.
They scattered without a moment's delay;
Every one of them threw down his lance—
The Turkmens and Caspian Alans,   1995
Like the Turks of Asia Minor,
Had not the courage to go on with the fight,
For Robert was all set for them
Wherever they tried to remain,
As they would be expected to do.   2000
Nowhere did they dare effect a brief halt;
They had already felt so many blows to the head,
So many death-dealing hits and so many wounds,
That bright red blood was streaming all over.
They fled so fast and furiously   2005
That the Romans couldn't catch even one
They might hold as a prize or for ransom.
Following Robert, one after another,
They ran after the Turks to put them to death
And stop all their braying and shouting.   2010
Down to the sea the pursuit went on—
Oh, the Turks' deadly defeat!
They never glanced at their tents:
More pressing matters were now on their minds!

They had no time to pull down   2015
Their pavilions or pack up their goods
Or gather their sails or cart off their clothes.
Downcast, dejected, forlorn,
They attempted to swim in the sea.
God! How they'd have loved to have horses   2020
To carry them out to their ships!
It was a terrible setback
Not to know how to swim,
For the Romans did not stop clubbing
Their limbs and their brains;   2025
Twenty thousand they left dead
On the shore, apart from the men
Who had lost their lives for want of the skill
To swim out to their ships;
They were doomed, indeed, to perish at sea,   2030
Ten thousand such creatures or more,
Who would never, in city or town,
Be part of the crowd.

When Robert saw his pursuit at an end
And everyone running to pick up the booty,   2035
He, with no wish to take part in the rush,
Backed away from the field and vanished instead,
So that no man in the throng gathered there
Could have any idea of his fate.
He quickly returned to the envoy of God,   2040
Waiting to greet him at the fountain he knew.
Had he been at a quintain drill,
His shield, held together by rigid tacks,
Could not have been more thoroughly pierced,
Nor his helmet more perfectly battered   2045
Had it been mounted
On sharp-pointed stakes or on a post
For training to withstand heavy hits from an axe.
From the blows he'd sustained on his nasal,
His whole visage was crimson with blood;   2050
Links of mail had bitten his face,

And the marks of their bites were apparent.
There was no counting the blows he'd sustained.
He dismounted in the shadows of a stream
And disarmed with no hesitation,   2055
Then put on the clothes he'd been wearing before.
God's envoy, impatient to leave,
Found his way back
With all the arms and equipment he'd brought
To open the way to Robert's great feats.   2060
As he had come, so did he leave,
Glad to have seen the triumph achieved.

Robert, whose face was all bloodied,
Hurried right up to the spring.
He washed around all his wounds,   2065
But the scratches and scrapes
That covered his face
Stood out more clearly as a result.
Once he had washed in the stream,
He descended to rest   2070
Under the stairs in the chapel;
He piled up some straw to lie down;
Robert, saintly man, rested his head
And fell right to sleep in perfect repose.

The damsel sitting at the window   2075
Saw all that had happened
And everything Robert had done;
She saw how he had faced down the Turks
And brought all their troops to defeat;
She saw how then he returned   2080
To the spring under the tree
—The spring colder than marble—
And how he surrendered his weapons;
She saw how he washed his bloodstained face
In the stream at the fountain.   2085
The young lady, who was hardly a dolt,
Thought he must be a man of high station

To have hidden his person for so long a duration.

N ow I should like to go back for a moment
   To bring the war to its proper conclusion.   2090
Roman forces on the shore
Inflicted on the Turks such remarkable losses
As to have slain one third of their men
And taken rich admirals captive;
They seized goods and took money,   2095
Silver and gold and pavilions and tents,
Horses and mules and finely wrought vessels.
The Romans gathered whatever they found
And presented it all the Emperor
With the wish and the hope   2100
That he would proceed as he chose,
But not overlooking the abundant rewards
Due the sword-flashing, lance-wielding knight
Who it actually was, with his weapons of steel,
That had shown them the way to the Turks   2105
And alone led the chase to defeat them for all.

Said the Emperor, "He shall have all!
Indeed, no riches he might want
Would I fail to accord him,
For he is the bold man and brave   2110
Who came to our aid in direst need.
His merest desire is my command,
And I shall deny him nothing he wishes.
Go find me the man; this is your mission!"

T hen they searched for the knight,   2115
   Seeking and asking wherever they could,
But they heard not a word
In response to their quest.
The Emperor was informed of their failure
And felt deeply pained and upset   2120
Never to have seen whoever he was,
Never to have met him or known him at all.

Since no one had heard even hints of his name,
They all thought, inside the court and without,
That he had to have been some friend of the Lord,   2125
Divinely dispatched to the field
To defend the honor of Rome,
For no ordinary man, no man of flesh,
Could have waged such a battle as he had done:

"He is a knight of Christ Jesus,   2130
And he has returned whence he came;
No finer miracle has ever occurred
In all the years of the city of Rome."

There was great jubilation among all the people;
The Emperor wept tears of joy: 2135
I think the court had never seen
So jubilant an Emperor.
Then he mounted, the Emperor did,
On his many-hued charger.
Noble nature and goodness   2140
Urged him ahead to a generous deed:
He came to the grandest barons of Rome
And said to them all
That for love of the Lord
He wished them to grant him the favor   2145
That very same day
Of coming to dine at his table.
They were pleased to accept.
For love of the King most high,   2150
He invited the Pope as well,
To dine with him on the same afternoon,
And the Pope made no move to decline.
The stewards who served at the court
And the servants who waited at table
Rushed about, preparing the service   2155
As the Emperor ordered;
He paused not long to partake of the feast,
Then ordered the war's winnings be brought

And he offered the barons most of that wealth;
Only a small part did he keep for himself.   2160

I n Rome the news came
To the ladies and damsels
And maidens at court
—Who had been terribly worried—
That the Turks were defeated   2165
And driven away
By one knight alone,
A knight richly equipped with arms
That were gleaming more brightly
Than ice on branches in winter.   2170
It was agreed throughout the city
That he who had shown proof of such prowess
Must have been sent by the heavenly King.
Rome was filled with frenzied rejoicing,
With jubilant noise,   2175
But by far the most festive of storms
Came from the sharp tolling of bells
That resounded through vaults and crenelles.

T he Romans reentered the city
With the Emperor and all of his barons,   2180
To cries of great joy and delight
And with music sounding all through the palace.
They dismounted in a riot of pleasure
—As the chronicle tells us—
And the Pope was very much of the party.   2185
Once they'd removed their battle attire,
These men so well exercised
Donned very different apparel:
Luxurious garments, magnificent robes.
Then came the news   2190
That the feast was all ready.
The Emperor called for the water
And, as ever of generous heart,
Asked that the Pope be first at the ewer

And then had him placed first at the table, 2195
Before even himself—which is no lie!
Then he sent for his beautiful daughter,
Who always brought joy to his heart;
He had her seated beside him
In the loveliest place he could see. 2200
Then came the turn of the barons—
Not a thief or a robber among them,
For all, indeed, were proper counts,
So no shame attached to that table!
The flower of knighthood 2205
And all the young nobles
Sat below on the floor.
They were all served a splendid
And copious feast,
With great platters of meats 2210
And sweetly spiced wines,
Mulberry brews and mulled ciders so fine!

When Robert woke up,
He hurt badly all over;
He lifted his head, which like his face 2215
Bore the marks of multiple wounds.
Risen, he went to the great banquet hall,
But he didn't go hopping or dancing,
Which immense fatigue forbade.
He walked up to the Emperor. 2220
As soon as the beautiful maiden beheld him,
She rose from her place in greeting;
In the presence of all at the table,
She made a deep bow with her head.
When she had shown this sign of respect, 2225
She returned with good grace to her seat
Beside her father, the Emperor.
He, for his part, was nonplussed and embarrassed,
Not knowing why she'd behaved in this way;
He declined, though, to seek a prompt explanation. 2230
There was consternation enough at the banquet;

Wicked tongues and knavish spirits
Had much too much to say;
They took the girl for demented
So to have honored the court's dumb fool.   2235
Robert, with no hesitation
And with no sign of confusion, sat down.
The Emperor peered at his face
For a moment and saw the marks
That a hauberk must have made;   2240
He saw the eyebrows swollen thick,
Skinned down to the bone,
And the nose that had been crushed,
Smashed and broken in the middle.
The Emperor's heart burst with rage   2245
And in his anger he had this to say:

"There are many in this city
All too guilty of injustice and iniquity.
God curse the cowards
—Too countless all over by far!—   2250
Who, it's clear, wronged me deeply
By beating my jester to an inch of his death.
While we were away, defending our city,
Ruffians led him to stray far afield
And forced him into a hauberk;   2255
The scratches and marks of the mail on his flesh
Still appear very fresh."

"My lord," said those who were present,
"Let it be! It's of little importance!
He fought his battle   2260
Just as we fought ours—
He felt the heat just as we did!"

The Emperor replied, "I cannot bear
To have anyone strike him or touch him.
If you witnessed his stunts   2265
And his wonderful capers,

You too could hardly stop laughing."

The Pope spoke and said, "Dear sir,
Do let us see one of his capers!"

The Emperor whispered to the steward   2270
Who was standing close by
That he should give some food
To the greyhound in front of the fool.
The order was immediately followed.
The greyhound was thrown a fistful of morsels   2275
That were cut into very small pieces.
Robert ran toward the dog
And seized them right from his jaw,
Then chewed them calmly,
With no show of distaste or of triumph.   2280
Everyone laughed, young and old;
Even tired old men who'd seen it all
Enjoyed the show and laughed.
All through the palace, people said
They had never before seen so funny a fool.   2285
The maiden, however, by what she heard
Was pained and perturbed; her heart felt a wound
But she didn't know what she could do.

W hen the tablecloths were removed
    And the banquet tables moved to the side,   2290
Talk turned to the unknown knight and they all said   2291
How sorry they were not to have identified him.   2291a
God! How ready he'd been
To show courage and prowess!
The Emperor, with his noble concern
For dignity and honor,   2295
Praised the white-shielded knight
Who had accomplished so wondrous a feat:
If he had been a wolf and the Turks only sheep,
They would not have faced a more formidable foe;
He never encountered an enemy troop so fierce   2300

That he couldn't bring it to heel in a trice.

"May God never grant my soul salvation,"
  Said the great, gallant Emperor,
"If the knight ever made himself known
  And I failed to make him a duke or a count!   2305
  Did he not save me from shame
  And from ruin and loss?
  I would reward him with all that I owe him,
  If only he deigned to appear in my court!"

At that point, the maiden could hardly hold back   2310
  From making her father a sign
  That there, in his presence,
  Was the knight whom he meant,
  Who in battle had been so triumphant.
  Stammering and stuttering,   2315
  The beautiful damsel tried to speak to her father,
  But he found her sounds beyond comprehension.
  The girl was wildly upset,
  Pointing to the jester to say what she wanted;
  The Emperor was no less disturbed,   2320
  Troubled and angered and deeply perplexed,
  Because never yet had he seen her
  Behave anywhere in so frantic a way.
  He turned to a valet of his
  Whom he told to summon her ladies.   2325
  They came, and he asked them
  To explain the girl's gestures:
  He needed to know just what she meant
  By the signs she was making.

"Of course, my lord," they replied.   2330

With gestures, they put the question
  To their charge and, with gestures,
  They told her to show what she had done;
  The noble young lady, unable to talk,

Signed her reply to explain   2335
In all truth what she meant;
Gestures exchanged were signs understood!
One of the ladies had a good laugh
And said to the Emperor,

"My lord," she said, "what I've just learned   2340
Is amazing and puzzling:
My lady maintains that the fool is more precious
Than anyone else from here to Mamistra!"

"Indeed," said the other,
"She says much more than just that!   2345
This morning, when you crossed
The woods onto the plain
And planted your flag,
Your daughter, to see you,
Went to sit at her window,   2350
Which looks down at the fountain.
Under the pine in that spot,
She noticed the jester with his hands out to God,
Then saw ride up, without a moment's delay,
A man in full armor, who then dismounted.   2355
She had no trouble hearing his words;
He commanded the jester to arm
And, once he had the shield at his neck,
The maiden saw him rush into battle.
It is he—there's no doubt—   2360
Who defeated the Turks!
The valiant knight that you seek is the jester himself—
So claims your dear and beautiful daughter.
Here is something else she reports:
When the battle was over,   2365
He came back past the hedge,
Armed and astride his white charger;
Down there, at the spring,
He returned all the armor to the unknown provider,
Who then rode away in a hurry   2370

With all his equipment still gleaming and white.
Then the fool went to the spring
To wash all the blood from his face.
That is what the dear maiden witnessed,
What her eyes saw and what she relates; 2375
That's what her gestures dictate."

The Emperor exclaimed, "This is fantastic;
I have never heard anything like it!
I always thought my dear daughter
Was the courtliest damsel, 2380
The brightest by far, the most sensible
Anywhere in the world.
And now she turns out to be a born fool
And so brainless a dolt
That I wish she had died in the womb! 2385
Do you know why she so cares for the jester?
Because he can't talk!
My dolt of a daughter
Is in love with the fellow mute that he is!
Among all the sayings that the *vilain* records 2390
Is a proverb that applies well to this case:
Birds of a feather flock together.
My daughter is drunk; take her away!
Take her to her room right away
And don't let her out of your sight! 2395
Tell her—and make it clear—
That she is never to pay further heed
To the jester and never again attend to his case.
She offended me grossly
When she rose to acknowledge the fool! 2400
That's when I saw she was mad—
That she desired the jester and lusted for him."

The ladies then led the maiden away
And did what they could to teach her a lesson.
The Pope, for his part, 2405
Took his leave, and the guests all departed.

Robert returned to his bed of fresh straw
To sleep through the night with the dogs.

S o the Turks sailed away,
  Confused and defeated, out to the sea.   2410
They had a fine wind for sailing
With no need to be on the sea very long.
They returned to their country,
Each man to the place of his birth.
They groaned and howled loudly   2415
As they thought of the men the Romans had slain
And they shed countless tears as they wept.
Through pagan lands their laments were soon heard.
The princes who ruled all those places,
As soon as the news came to them   2420
Of the terrible triumph of Rome
And the dreadful defeat their kinfolk had suffered,
All pledged one to another
And swore by their gods
To return right away to the Romans   2425
And avenge the deaths of their kin
While weather and wind were still in their favor.
They would make them pay dearly
For all of that carnage, those Romans,
Those people they hated beyond any others!   2430
They transmitted their plans
To their friends and allies,
Who, all of them, welcomed this war of revenge.
Since it presented a great hazard and peril,
It demanded preparation and care.   2435
They repaired and restored all their ships
And built vessels and barges
And riggings and very broad scows
And large, many-oared galleys.
Once the season was right, their forces were ready,   2440
With twice the manpower they'd originally had.
From one place and another, by various routes,
Saracens came to be part of the army.

They loaded their vessels as quickly
As possible, not wasting a moment.   2445
They boarded the ships and set out to sea,
Then went forth all sails unfurled;
Guided by day by the sun and at night by the stars,
They arrived at Rome's port in the shortest of time.
The Arabs and Caspian Comans   2450
And the Turks from Khorasan
And the city of Nirvana
Pitched their tents on the beach.
To Rome the news soon came
Of the arrival of the Turks—   2455
Not a small and secret landing,
But a broad display of might
That ranged along the whole front of the sea.
A serious threat to the Romans they were,
For no fear could dampen their zeal   2460
To avenge all the deaths of their kin,
Deaths that had brought them pain and chagrin.

R ome was now fearfully frightened.
    At the Emperor's command,
Word was sent to the seneschal,   2465
Along with a promise of payment
If he but came right away to the aid
Of those trying to save the great city
From the Turks determined to raze it.
He replied that instead he would aid in the razing   2470
Unless he were granted the girl
Who had sparked in his heart
A fire of still unextinguished desire.
Oh, the affront to his Emperor and sire!

T he messengers returned   2475
    And to their lord reported
That the seneschal would only repeat his demand
That he grant him his dear, lovely daughter.
The Emperor, in a fury, swore by God

That, as long as he had life in his veins,   2480
He would never to that man surrender the girl;
It would stain and dishonor all that was Rome!
Never, please God, would that shame occur,
Nor would there be further talk of the matter.
Yes, there would be a high price to pay!   2485
Then at his palace he assembled
His council of barons
Who owed him allegiance.
They discussed at great length
All the issues   2490
And arrived at the same understanding:
God, who had not failed them before,
Would help them in this battle, too.
He never forsakes those faithful to him!
With that thought he sent them great comfort.   2495
They would all have been vanquished and slain
If God had not sent them
The man who had served as their friend and ally,
Whose lance proved their foes' great undoing.
With strong, earnest faith in the Lord,   2500
He would help them again
To defeat all those pagans seeking revenge.

Deliberations concluded at last,
And the council named the day they would move
Contra the Turks, who were pressing them badly,   2505
Plundering farms and wreaking devastation,
Inflicting great harm on the people of Rome.
Young and old, both women and men,
All fasted and prayed and made many a vow.
The priests turned the Mass into heartfelt prayer,   2510
Beseeching the Lord with uncountable tears
To send them, as he had once before,
The valiant knight whose bright, gleaming arms
Had let them avert untellable harm.

But first, one early Monday morning,   2515
The Turks, bemoaning the notion
That their vengeance had stalled,
Set out toward the city in tightly closed ranks,
Ready for disciplined combat.
First to march forth were the plumed and the smartest,   2520
The boldest and most capable men,
Who had no inclination to treat the Romans
With kindness when they'd find them on the field;
Indeed, they couldn't dream of finer prey!
Clouds of dust reached the eyes   2525
Of Roman captains, who took fright
And rushed to arms as fast as they could.
The Emperor was the first
To dress himself in armor, fearing the worst
And letting tears mixed with sweat   2530
Run down the length of his face.
He laced on his helmet when astride his mount.
He arranged and readied all battalions
And assigned the constables to their troops
In the way that was proper,   2535
So they'd not be surprised by the Saracen foe.
When all were prepared, they moved onto the field
On their loud and whinnying horses,
As the long trumpets were sounding;
In the brilliance of sunshine,   2540
Their shields glittered and flashed,
While their pennants and banners flapped in the wind.
Ladies and damsels,
Young girls and maidens,
Wept heavy tears for their loved ones   2545
In grave danger of dying,
And they prayed to our heavenly Lord
That he bring to their aid
The knight with the gleaming sword.
That was the prayer of all noble ladies.   2550
The Emperor went without waiting
To take leave of his daughter.

He kissed her gently and wept.

"Daughter," he said, "don't be afraid,
For God will not fail to come to our aid;   2555
He will be with us in battle."

He stayed no longer, but left.
The maiden sighed and she wept.
She went upstairs to her window
To have a clear view of the whole field of battle.   2560

Now is the time to tell you more about Robert.
No grief could be greater than his
When he witnessed the Emperor
Departing from Rome with fear in his heart.
Happily would he have helped him,   2565
If God had but granted him leave;
He knew not what to do or to say;
He let his eyes shed tears and his heart heave sighs.
To give way to his pain, he entered the garden.
All alone, no one else to be seen,   2570
He sat down at the fountain.
There, by himself, he rested and wept,
Crying to God for his mercy,
Hands joined in prayer—
But only in thought, for he said not a word.   2575
Lo! Now there appeared the divine emissary,
Shining again in his gleaming white armor.
Under the pine with its broad green branches,
He dismounted onto the grass of the meadow.
The heart of the maiden quickened with joy,   2580
For now she knew with no doubt
That the knight would enter the battle
Who had valor and prowess equal to none.
What elation she felt in her heart!

"Robert, my friend," said God's envoy,   2585
Who was courtly and winsomely keen,

"God commands that you arm right away!"

Robert obeyed without any delay.

A rmored and astride his fine steed,
He rode past the break in the hedge   2590
Down to the plain outside;
To the spot where he heard the bright sound of horns
He headed his horse and his white-pennoned lance.
Already the Turks had pursued
Across a wide stretch of land   2595
Romans who knew only to retreat and to run.
Their rout was sure and certain —
When suddenly they stopped to turn 'round,
For in the distance they espied
Their Robert, racing to their rescue.   2600
Ah, God! The thrill they then felt!
They took heart—they felt brave—had courage again.
The Emperor was filled with relief and with joy,
And the Pope, Holy Father, was joyful no less.
The Turks, for their part, at the sight   2605
Of white arms, recognized Robert as well.
From the moment they saw him,
The boldest and bravest were worried;
Hadn't they heard lengthy tales of the knight
Whose lance and bright sword had martyred so many!   2610
Now he went for their throats and their chests;
They thought they were seeing Saint George
And trembled with terror and fright.
Meanwhile, Robert found the army of Romans
In thorough disorder and prepared for defeat   2615
If their confusion went on for another short while;
But the appearance of Robert
Gave them new strength,
And they gathered back all the scattering men.
Nothing but a tempest of deafening power   2620
Could have unleashed such thunderous rage
As did Robert, attacking the Turks.

With daring and prowess,
He threw his horse headlong
Into the thick of the battle   2625
Where he spotted the head of their troops.
No one could stop him
From rushing with hurricane force
Into the midst of the enemy ranks.
At his approach, the Turks collapsed in confusion;   2630
He raced ahead and attacked their head man;
He struck him straight on with his sword,
Sending the blade right through his ribs
And downing him lifeless right there
In front of all his companions.   2635
Robert then fell on those dogs, those Turks,
Wherever he found them;
He speared so many brains
And slew so many fighters with his lance
That the Turks recoiled in terror   2640
And didn't have the courage to respond.
With that, the Romans, not pausing to rest,
Attacked the Turks, following Robert's example;
Those he unhorsed they fed to their swords;
They found plenty to do,   2645
For Robert could hardly deliver a blow
Without flinging his man down to the ground.
Now the Turks faced the worst of the war
And were shocked to the quick by their rout.
They felt forced into flight, whatever their number;   2650
They couldn't fight back on the field
And they dared not grant Robert more time,
For he's what they feared more than anything else.
His performance that day was better by half
Than it had been the previous time.   2655
He fought to such stunning effect
That the point of his sword
Cleared the whole field of its Turkish invaders.
He drove them back into total collapse
Amid the howls and the shouts of pursuit.   2660

The Saracens thought not to tarry;
Emirs or admirals or merely great lords,
They fled in utter confusion,
And captives had no chance to seek ransom.
Into the sea their fright took them fleeing,   2665
And no waves were too high or too wild
To stop them from trying to swim.
They wept for their women and children,
For many knew they'd not see them again;
They drowned in the filth of their frightened bowels.   2670
They gave no thought to folding their tents
Or to saving whatever they owned;
No, that day such concerns didn't touch them.
There were not even half who failed to escape
Being slain on the ground   2675
Or pushed to their death in the water.
While the Romans were intent
On striking the Turks and claiming their heads
And on rapidly carting the booty away
From the pavilions that were theirs now to pillage,   2680
Robert set out on his silent way,
Undisturbed and unquestioned.
Several men saw him go down
To the little wood
At some remove from the city.   2685

Through the breach that we know
He passed into the orchard
Where the gentle stream flowed.
He found God's envoy expecting him there,
Who bade him be quick to remove all his armor,   2690
Lest anyone take notice.
Robert, with no wish to be seen,
Removed arms and armor as bidden.
All equipment but his lance
He returned to the envoy, who turned on his heels   2695
And stayed no more in the garden,
Leaving Robert alone.

His face, discolored and covered with blood
And scratched by the blows he'd received,
He went, experienced now,   2700
To bathe at the fountain
Whose water was flowing nearby.
Then he went to the chapel and fell fast asleep.
The damsel witnessed the scene
From the window, where she once again sat.   2705
She was moved by compassion
And the tears of her eyes streamed down her cheeks.
She rose from her seat at the window
And walked down the stairs
In search of relief anywhere.   2710

The Emperor, once the field
Had fallen to him,
With the Saracens disgraced and defeated,
Made this pronouncement,
Giving voice to his plan: 2715

"I have a champion," he said,
"A defender who has saved and protected me
And restored my imperial power:
Bring him forth at this instant,
So I may name him my friend!"   2720

Just as the Emperor had ordered,
The man was immediately summoned,
But no one known at the court or even outside
Could find any sign of the person.
They were all disappointed   2725
To have seen him nowhere.
The Emperor was plunged into gloom;
The Pope and men of the law, for their part,
Were baffled and glum.

"He had no wings and could hardly have flown!"   2730

This was said by the men
Who had seen and recalled him
As he'd entered the wood not far from the city,
Making his way like anyone else,
Walking ahead like any man they might know.   2735
But where he was going
Or lived or intended to stay,
Now back from the battle, they couldn't say.

The Emperor said, "He is gone.
We shall never again be so close   2740
To seeing him or his face.
What is lost is lost,
And that is how it has to be.
Everyone should now return home,
But I want all the barons   2745
And the stalwart, noble knights
To come to my table to mark this victorious day
And hold it in thought forever.
My lord, the Pope, will be there as well."

They all voiced their assent, with no disagreement.   2750
They took then the road back to Rome
And returned amid great jubilation.
They stopped to give thanks to Saint Peter,
Then proceeded to dine
At the Emperor's great table,   2755
Where they could hear the songs of his players.
The trumpet announced the moment to wash
As the kitchen help started
To lay out the platters of food.
The Pope washed his hands,   2760
Then went to sit at the table
In the choicest place he could see.
The Emperor, beaming with pleasure,
Sent for his beautiful daughter.
The maiden removed the constraint of her wimple   2765
And sat down alongside her father;

Their table stood several steps above all the rest.
Then came the counts and the dukes
And then the barons of Rome.
On the main level, the hall was now filled 2770
With the region's fine knights,
All those men ever ready for war.
They took their seats through the room
On benches that no one disputed.
When the platters began to arrive, 2775
The Emperor thought it time for some quiet,
Because the noise was too great.
It took but a moment for the din to abate.

Meanwhile, under the stairs,
Robert awoke, terribly tired 2780
And battered and scratched,
For the Turks had dealt harshly with him.
He went for some food to the great hall of the banquet,
Where he quietly entered with no one to stop him.
The Emperor had no sooner seen him come in 2785
Than he cried in his bright and powerful voice,

"How welcome you are, my good man!
Welcome, you wise and quick-witted lord!
Come here and sit down
In the most comfortable seat that you see! 2790
Your arrival, I tell you,
Means the party goes on!"

Robert sat down at the Emperor's feet.
But listen to what the damsel, his daughter, then did!
She rose to her feet in front of the fool 2795
To honor his valor, to honor his prowess and power;
She bowed her blond head, then sat again,
Not showing the slightest discomfort.
The Emperor, for his part, was deeply embarrassed,
But, eager to keep a proper appearance, 2800
Preferred not to show displeasure or shame,

So he turned his attention to a different topic:
He spoke of his jester, who was obviously wounded.

"God!" he exclaimed, "Look what they've done
To my fool! Look how people have bruised   2805
And battered his face!"

Then he ordered his servants
To bring out food in abundance
Which they did without stinting.
Knowing how Robert proceeded,   2810
They served the food to the dog;
Robert then pounced and pushed him away;
He relied on no stick, no weapon at all,
To snatch the food from the jaws of the hound.
Then he chewed and he swallowed with pleasure   2815
As much of the food as he liked,
And when he was sated
And his hunger was stilled,
He offered the dog the delicious remains,
Letting him take them right from his mouth.   2820
Young and old found this all a delight;
Everyone present
Enjoyed the wonderful show,
Remarking they'd never seen a jester that good
Anywhere closer than far to the south.   2825
After the meal, the cloths were removed
By the servants who had that particular task;
The tables were pushed to a side and were stacked.

The young men, after dinner,
Gathered together in a well-ordered line   2830
To stand before their Emperor.
Eloquent speakers among them
Told how the Emperor and indeed all of Rome
Owed their success to one man alone,
The man in white armor, bearing arms all of white: 2835
Was it not he who had slain all the pagans?

"You are speaking the truth," the Emperor agreed.
"All the booty of war would surely be his
If he deigned to come forth with a claim;
And I would give him a great part of my land,   2840
Along with much of my treasure,
If only he wanted to have it—
But it seems clear he has no care for rewards.
I don't know what mysterious cause
Brings him this year once more to our aid   2845
Yet stops him from all explanation;
I would pay him a thousand marks of fine gold
And would gladly give him much more than that,
If he but once allowed me to face him
Right here, with no helmet hiding his face."   2850

His daughter, when hearing these words,
Could not hold her peace any longer.
Mute as before, she pointed to Robert
And made a strange sign to her father,
Which the Emperor did not understand.   2855
He then called for the ladies
Who *would* understand what she wanted to say:
The girl surely knew something
That she wanted to tell him!
The ladies appeared,   2860
Kind governesses all,
And the eldest among them, the grayest of heads,
Didn't take long to divine her intention.

The good woman spoke, "Emperor, my lord,
What your daughter desires to tell you   2865
Holds no interest whatever.
She claims that your jester, a madman since birth,
Freed the whole country
From the hands of the Turks;
He is the one who vanquished them all,   2870
The valiant knight armored in white!
He acquired his arms under the branches

Of the pine that inclines over the spring;
His was the standard and his was the shield
That won you your triumph in battle.   2875
Such is her claim—pure whimsy or worse!
She says that his face is all mauled,
Injured and wounded and bruised
By the terrible blows he received
As he fought back the foe."   2880

"Stop right there!" cried the Emperor;
"I won't hear one more word!
What you tell me, my ladies, is rubbish!
My daughter is mad—
All the madder for that fool   2885
With whom she is smitten;
And because he speaks no more
Than my speechless fool of a daughter,
She is wildly besotted by him.
No, she has lost all control of her senses.   2890
Take her away now (may hellfire burn her!)
And take care that you watch her more closely
Than you have done hitherto;
It sorely offends me
To hear her rave so intently!"   2895

The ladies, with no word of resistance,
Led the maiden away,
The valorous, virtuous, sensible maid.
The barons tarried no longer,
But bade good night to the Emperor   2900
And went their various ways:
A proper end to a memorable day.

The Turks, for their part, sailed back right away,
      Shedding tear upon tear
For the friends they had lost   2905
On the field before Rome, the city they'd wanted.
Mourning and grief left them craving revenge.

They sailed and pushed on
Till they came, near the plain of Romaine,
To a populous, prosperous city. 2910
They lamented the great harm they had suffered,
And telling the tale to allies
Sharpened their pain and heightened their wrath.
When listeners heard how their martyrs
Had suffered such infamous treatment, 2915
Turks from Babylon in the desert,
Like those from Macedonia
And from that other Babylon in Egypt,
Streamed together, armed and prepared.
Never, they threatened, by night nor by day, 2920
Would they rest until they'd avenged
The disgrace that had shamed them at Rome.
Syrian men and Arabian men,
Men bristly bearded, with hair standing on end,
Were drawn to the rally 2925
Held for great crowds at Valona;
Alexandrian Turks were there in large numbers,
As were men from warm Spain and frost-covered Rus
And Camela and the land all around.
The king of Damascus did not run from his duty, 2930
But assembled his numerous barons
To avenge all the Turks of the Caspian coast.
From Edessa and Persian Khorasan
And other lands far and near,
The Turks all gathered together 2935
And resolved in a heated great council
To go sack the city of Rome.
Other troops from the Caspian region
Joined forces with them.
Their vessels were varied and different, 2940
But equipped and outfitted in sumptuous fashion.
Never before had a Saracen host put to sea
As tremendous a fleet as assembled this time
Or as the eldest of men had seen in their lives.
Those devils of Turks swore by the God 2945

Of their faith that, if they lived long enough
To drop anchor off Rome,
The Romans would all be slain and destroyed—
Those Romans who had handed their people
A defeat like no other.   2950
Above all, however, the man wielding white weapons
Would enjoy no protection from magical spells!
Should he emerge on the field, then—by God!—
They would rip his soul right out of his body!

Now did the Turks start under way;   2955
Let it freeze; let it pour; they were not to be stopped!
They called too for the aid of non-Turkish friends,
Sending their runners
To the farthest, most foreign of realms,
Asking for masses of men   2960
Well armed and equipped—
But the answers that came were shrugs of disdain:
They would surely be martyred
If they took all such forces to Rome!
In the season when green returns to the fields   2965
And leaves reappear with new buds,
The pagans set sail on a blustery sea,
Its waves reaching high with threatening winds.
But they sailed and pushed on,
Those treacherous, devilish Turks,   2970
Until they arrived at the redoubtable port
Where they'd seen their companions go down;
Eight leagues were they now from the city of Rome.
The Saracens then, those detestable men,
Spilled out of their ships in a rush;   2975
They set up their tents and pavilions
And unloaded their vessels
With no waiting.

The news quickly came to the city
That the Turks had arrived at the shore,   2980
Quietly ready to fight,

And that the host they'd assembled
Was greater by far than the two vanquished
And shamed in the earlier battles.
Now were the Romans so terribly frightened   2985
They had never yet felt such remarkable fear;
They trembled as never before.
The Emperor was thoroughly shaken
By the news he'd just heard.
He sent out the word to all parts of the realm   2990
That Rome needed help and defending,
For the Turks were a mortal and imminent threat.
To the seneschal he sent word once again
That he expected a pledge of support
And his presence beside him in battle: 2995
He mustn't, by God, fail him now in his fight
'Gainst the Turks of Romaine—
Which would be a gross and culpable error!
The seneschal was unmoved by the Emperor's appeal.
He swore by God and his Mother   3000
That he would never come to his aid
Unless and until the Emperor agreed
To grant him his daughter as wife.
The Emperor replied he was not in the habit
Of offering pearls to fat pigs.   3005
Better the people of Rome come to perish
And the walls of the city crumble to dust
Than he yield him his daughter!
So the seneschal stood apart from the battle
(For which many a Roman rebuked him).   3010
The Emperor gathered his army
And the Romans undertook a great fast
To beg God for good counsel,
While the ladies of Rome held a vigil,
Praying to God that he send them   3015
Their winning defender,
The knight of the gleaming white shield,
Thanks to whom they'd survived until now—
For doubtless they'd have died long ago

If not for his stand against their pitiless foe.   3020

N ow was the Emperor prepared to go fight;
   He was eager, moreover, not to be scorned
For letting the Turks make the first move:
He wanted to show his defense was all ready.
On a Wednesday at daybreak,   3025
The Saracens were preparing
To engage with the Romans.
Troops from the Caspian coast
Formed the leading battalion,
And then came another.   3030
—But my tale is already too long,
   So I'll cite no more than a number or two:
How many Turkish divisions there were
And how many men they contained—
There were four and twenty battalions   3035
That went forth to wage war on the Romans,
And in each there were ten thousand men.
They posed a great threat to the city,
For they were eager for mayhem and blood.
From the arcades at the top of those heavenly walls,   3040
The sentinels saw them approaching,
And everyone heard the loud notes of their trumpets
And the sound of their horns.
The Emperor wasted no time
To alert the good Pope, whom he escorted now   3045
Into the hall, which was filled
With high barons of the land all around,
For whom war was a fact and familiar event.
In view of the urgency that all of them felt,
They withdrew to a chamber to take counsel   3050
And determine what their plan would now be.
They needed to see what action they'd take:
How they would march into battle,
How they'd safeguard the land that was theirs
When faced with the fast-moving Turks.   3055
Their discussion at length moved on to these words,

The terms of the Emperor, who said,

"My lords," he began, "our Father in Heaven
Twice sent to us here
A remarkable knight whose protection   3060
Allowed us to fend off the Turks,
Whose assault we could hardly repel by ourselves.
Rome would long since have been crushed
If not for the strength and the struggle
Of the white-armored knight and his brilliant defense.   3065
Now I shall tell you the thought in my mind.
The man who twice has served me so well
Deserves a resounding reward,
Which I hope he will care to accept.
If once more he appears, as he has done in the past,   3070
To help us this time, I'll make sure not to miss him;
I want very much to reward
His exceptional service,
For he spares no trouble or effort.
If he is a man sent us by God,   3075
. . .
We can only be grateful and glad
And admit he is beyond our reach;
But if he's a man of this world,
Nothing shall stop me   3080
From catching him before he departs—
Provided he'll have come to the battle!
As soon as I'm armed,
I'll choose thirty good knights
To hide in the shade of the trees   3085
Down there in the plain near the thicket.
Servants and other such people
Have told me he passes that way
When he sees that the fighting is over.
The knights will jump out and will seize him—   3090
If it please God to bring him to us!"

Everyone nodded, "May it be thus!"

At that, they all ran for their arms.
Many went with warm tears in their eyes
To take up their hauberks and helmets,   3095
Which, hauberks and all, they hoped would protect them.
Once they were armored and armed,
Every man, under the colorful plumes of his heaume,
Sighed and cried to our Lord
That, safely and with his equipment,   3100
He let him come home
And that he relieve all his grief
By defeating the infidel pagans.
The Emperor did all that it took
To make his combat successful.   3105
He began to arrange his battalions;
When all his men were in place
And his battle plans ready,
He told his barons to start under way
In the name of the glorious Martyr   3110
Who suffered passion and death
For our redemption.
They all marched out as one,
To the blare of the trumpets and horns.
The Pope, with a great entourage,   3115
Walked out to the field behind a large banner,
Blessing the men as he went—
All those Romans in need of his comfort.
The Emperor waited no longer.
To his beautiful, generous daughter   3120
He bade his good-bye, then turned away weeping,
Worried and mournful and sad—
A man advancing at risk
Right into his fight with the Turks.
Down he went to the battlefield, leading his men.   3125
(God keep him now from harm and from death!)
When Robert saw them all marching out
To engage with the Turks, who were not far away,
He felt immense sadness and pain
That he was not part of their effort.   3130

His heart was persuaded
That he could soon bring great woe
To the Turks, who were quickly advancing
And had ridden so far
That Roman guards were already their captives.   3135
The Emperor disposed all his men
As he had planned.
He assigned thirty knights
To the small wood where they'd be shaded;
They quickly dismounted and took their positions   3140
In the clearing under the branches:
If the white knight came along
To take command of the battle,
They would catch him upon his return,
As the Emperor had ordered.   3145
He himself did not stay there,
But went off to his fight
With the Turks, a foe that he feared:
They were a huge and frightening army,
Bold and brave, harsh fighters and hardy.   3150

Hear now what Robert decided to do:
He went to the fountain
To see whether perhaps
The divine creature would be there
Bearing the arms that he'd brought in the past.   3155
Under the sweet fragrant pine,
Robert sat down and wept tender tears.
He turned toward the east, imploring the heavens,
Softly murmuring his plea to our Lord,
His prayer that he send   3160
Once again his heavenly envoy.
Forthwith, he saw God's angel appear,
Bearing the white equipment he'd need.
Robert felt great reassurance—
As did the delicate damsel   3165
Who in her room at the window
Worried for Rome and her father,

Engaged in a bitter and deadly contention.
The envoy of God did not tarry,
But went up to Robert and gave him   3170
The armor and arms he had sought.
He was magnificent, handsome to see
As he mounted his Heaven-sent steed;
The valiant hero with so many virtues
Galloped off right away,   3175
Bidding good-bye to the one sent by the Lord,
Who wished him success with a sign of the cross.
He hastened toward the plain of the combat,
Passing alongside the thicket
Where were stationed under the foliage   3180
The thirty elite cavaliers
Who were now utterly silent,
Awaiting the moment he'd be back,
When, if they could, they would seize him for good.
Robert raced on, who would brook no delay.   3185
To his right he could see
The great battle unfolding,
With the Turks, from the start,
By far in the lead;
They had pushed back the Romans   3190
Along with their banner of gold and the dragon.
The Romans were driven to envisage defeat—
When from afar they descried
The white knight and saw
He was riding toward them with all possible speed.   3195
Every man raised his hands up to God
In thanks for the help he was sending.
The Emperor wept out of joy,
For he had no more fear
That his men might be scattered: 3200
The white knight was approaching,
And the Turks would lose all reason for boasting!

No, the Turks were not pleased:
They had heard quite a lot

About the hero of Rome and his unparalleled power.   3205
Every man did what he could
To protect and defend his own body
To withstand the onslaught by Robert,
Who rushed ahead with fanatical speed,
For he felt driven to enter   3210
The core of that damned pagan force,
Hurtling by, lashing out,
Thrusting his lance into hearts, into heads.
He wanted the feasts of the Turks
To be mournful affairs and not joyous.   3215
A hungry wolf lunging after his prey
Is not quicker to pounce
Than Robert, lance ready,
Darting after the Turks.
He struck one of them so that the man fell   3220
To the ground, bearded face down, thoroughly dead.
Robert veered back and hacked off his head.

He threw himself into the Saracen crowd,
Spurring into their midst
His impetuous, spirited horse;   3225
He struck and struck down, thrust and threw over,
Kicking away what his lance had just toppled;
His banner was twisted and spattered
And reddened with blood.
His remarkable weapon left a score of Turks slain,   3230
Others crushed or bloodily maimed.
He espied a king of the Moors
Leading forward a handsome battalion
With obvious intent to do harm
To the Romans, whom he detested so much   3235
He would gladly and coldly put them to death.
Robert ran up toward him,
Pushing his way through the ranks;
His lance, already bloody,
He pushed right through the chest into his heart   3240
And brought him down dead

From the croup of his horse.
But the shaft of Robert's lance splintered and broke!
He tore out the sword that hung by his side
And pushed through the throng, 3245
Slicing and slaying and crushing;
He scattered Turks as if they were flies;
Many he turned into quivering wrecks,
As he hit and he maimed and he crippled.
The field all around him 3250
Was covered with those he'd knocked down,
And the whole place reeked of flesh and of gore.
He felled and cut down so many a man
That his wrath was the dread of every last Turk—
Those damnable Turks, whom God hurt and destroy! 3255
Wherever he went, the way opened before him;
He looked forward and saw them make way;
Once his back, though, was turned,
They reached for their lances or axes
Or pulled out their swords. 3260
But Robert was able to turn around fast,
Never pausing or resting or trusting;
He raced ahead; he swung back to the rear;
His fight was relentless; he had no man to fear.

Reassured now, the Romans 3265
Watched Robert's deeds on the field
And acclaimed their man's exultation.
The Turks cursed the foe who had shamed them.
They had no recourse in the face of a fighter
For whom no troop existed, be it ever so fierce, 3270
That he could not overcome or disperse.
He so broke up the vanguard battalion
And crushed it so badly
That the Turks could only take flight.
The Romans followed hard on their heels, 3275
Creating more turmoil and noise
For the Turks and leaving them woefully frightened.
Oh, they felt their great loss!

For the Emperor's men then attacked
With such great ferocity as to strip them   3280
Of all but their pain and then dash them
Into the midst of another battalion,
Whose order they thus wholly disrupted.
They could hardly hold out for long,
For they were knocked out of line by the Romans,   3285
Who were vengefully bent on their city's defense.
Robert galloped forward,
Hitting the Turks and hurting them hard,
Chasing them fast from unit to unit.
He tracked them along their terrible route   3290
And butchered the dogs he could reach.
Those Saracens couldn't move fast enough
To escape the sharp taste of Robert's fine sword.
Restlessly striking, he led them on for a league,
While Roman horsemen followed his lead   3295
And let no admiral, emir, or whatever Saracen prince
Get by with his life.
Robert, who parted and scattered them,
Drove through one corps and another
Of the numberless Turks.   3300
His galloping was not done in vain:
Whenever he saw a Saracen standard,
He raced ahead, with no one to stop him;
Then, with a crowd and great troop
Of Turks rushing up,   3305
He threw down and stamped on their banner.
He didn't pause in attacking the Turks;
Indeed, he wielded his sword to make so many perish
That others hung back, afraid to come near,
While the Romans, galloping after,   3310
Struck their own blows into the mass.
From every side, they went after the Turks
And hammered them harshly.
Saracens' strength was starting to ebb
And so was their well-vaunted courage,   3315
For Robert attacked with such violent boldness

That all they could do was retreat;
They abandoned the field, running off
In defeat, vanquished and thoroughly routed.
Ah, God! What a price they did pay   3320
For their pride and outrageous ambition!
Now they were shamed by their foe's opposition.

M en in pursuit and loud battle cries
    Made it clear how hard hit were the Turks.
They ran in such painful disorder   3325
That even the boldest
Had no thought for cousin or brother,
Companion or master or father;
They all fled, each man for himself,
Knowing full well they could hope   3330
For no ransom if they were caught
By those in charge of the war.
For that reason, they fled helter-skelter;
Neither old soldiers nor young looked this way or that,
But all charged ahead,   3335
Running so fast, riding so fast
That soon they were far from their tents,
And the Romans had no other intention
Than to slay them and beat them
And drown them in the depths of the sea.   3340

Oh, the Turks were ill served
As their horses now failed them:
Their riders had worked them too hard,
So the mounts were played out and exhausted.
They tried heading toward Rome,   3345
But great heat and fatigue
And the weight of the men on their backs
Weakened the steeds beyond animation.
The mounts that survived
The Romans butchered and ate.   3350
As for the Turks, they pressed them so hard
That fewer than half remained still alive.

Unable to reach as far as the port,
Men met death here and there on the field.

Robert ran on ahead,   3355
Never tired of smiting and killing;
He detested the Turks
And barred their way to the sea
Along the great marsh it was hard to traverse.
No lion or werewolf   3360
Ever ravaged its prey
As did Robert that day,
Killing and smashing those Turks;
His sword was dripping with blood.
At the port, on the shore,   3365
He so punished the foe
As to pile corpse upon corpse without number.
The enemy army was now
In complete disarray,
And they faced a great slaughter   3370
When the Romans arrived,
So the Turks gave no thought
To defending their tents or finding fresh cover;
Indeed, every rock and outcropping
Served as a height for deliberate death.   3375
God, with what fury
The Romans now slaked their thirst for revenge!
Robert didn't dawdle, and the Turks knew it well:
He even chased them into the sea
When they had nowhere else they could go.   3380
Then a number pushed ahead
To escape being hit,
But that move gained them nothing,
For they entered the water
Just as a terrible wind   3385
Churned the sea to such an extent
That wave crashed upon wave,
Turning everything white with froth and with foam.
The Turks expecting to be saved by the sea

Had a dreadful surprise   3390
As its fury threw them against one another
And soon swallowed up that entire vile race.
Their ships were beyond being reached;
Their boats were flooded and tossed,
So they drowned and they died where they were.   3395
Nowhere could the Turks find rescue or safety;
Of the few who were left on the shore,
Not one, I believe, remained long alive,
As the arms of the Romans received them
Eager to drink the blood of their veins.   3400
This was the end; the Turks were all gone.
Robert first, then the forces of Rome,
Had wiped them all out;
No hope was left; this was their final, definitive rout.

When they had martyred all of the Turks   3405
  —A far more frightful event than I've said—
The Romans set out in quest of treasure and booty.
Robert, however, took no part in that hunt,
But turned his attention to other concerns.
He made his way softly away from the field   3410
Now securely acquired,
And headed back, he believed, unperturbed
By anyone who might have espied him.
He went along toward the thicket
Where waited the thirty knights   3415
Nestled unseen in the foliage.
They watched Robert depart from the troops
And quickly come up toward their post.
They wanted not to advance, though,
To catch and unseat him   3420
Until they could see him up close
And be sure of success;
Only then would they seize him.
In that way, they could be sure of not failing,
Since, if they didn't succeed   3425
In grasping his bridle to hold him,

They could kill his good steed
And thus stop him from racing away;
He was so close to their trap,
It would shame them to let him escape! 3430
They took to their saddles with no further delay
And prepared to seize Robert.
They dashed out from the edge of the wood
As Robert was passing alongside the pasture
That joined his path to the thicket. 3435
That's when they spurred and leapt out of hiding.

"We've got you, good man!" they shouted together.
"Today is the day of your great celebration!
Rome awaits you, please God!"

Robert said not a word, but kept very quiet. 3440
He beheld all those horsemen
With puzzled surprise;
He was taken aback and knew not what to do.
He was fearful of facing a problem,
Soon understanding that the men all too close 3445
Were there at the Emperor's command
In an effort to grant him great wealth
And a position of honor beside him.
But Robert wanted none of all that!
He knew all too well what would happen: 3450
If he were captured, he'd be deeply confounded,
For his story would then be revealed
And he could no more remain where he was.
He began to address to Lord God
A silent prayer that he save him 3455
And that none of the knights take him captive.
He spurred forth of a sudden, hurling mount
And himself straight toward the valley
As fast as he could possibly dash.
After him rose a great cloud of dust 3460
Coming from those in pursuit;
Again and again they lowered their lances,

Wanting to strike Robert's horse dead.
So long and hard did they run that their mounts
Were worn out and had to pause for a rest.   3465
They stopped to drink at a shallow pond—
That is, all but one, for the thirtieth knight
Continued alone by a solitary path.
His companions were left far behind
As he raced on ahead and soon almost grasped   3470
Robert's horse, his hand on the bridle,
But Robert slipped from his reach and rode on.
When the knight saw he wasn't succeeding,
While Robert went on with no need of a pause,
He decided to make a different attempt: 3475
To pay for this hunt, a steed's life would be spent!

He galloped after Robert with a vigorous dash.
Once arrived at his target, he pointed his lance
To strike at the horse,
Wanting to hit him between one strap and another   3480
To pierce his heart and thus kill him.
But he wasn't able to push the lance in
And point it in the intended direction:
He hit Robert instead, piercing his thigh.
The weapon went in up to the shaft;   3485
I am sure Robert had never felt so searing a pain
As he did at that moment.
But wound and pain failed to stop him:
He galloped ahead at full speed even so,
Hurting and hit and hunched over,   3490
Trying to stanch the puncture and tear
To stop blood from dripping to earth.
The man didn't rest who had caused this mistake;
He pulled out his lance,
All bloodied and splintered,   3495
Except that the head remained stuck
In the flesh of Robert's left thigh.
The injury stung and made movement distressful,
Impeded by the spearhead lodged deep in his flesh.

Robert didn't know what he could do.   3500
Still, he pressed forward,
Making haste as well as he could,
Till he reached the pine garden and gave up his horse.
He returned mount and all paraphernalia
To God's envoy, who bade him good-bye   3505
And soon disappeared.

Robert pulled himself up to the fountain
Slowly, with care and effort and pain.
He was grievously, unbearably injured.
He cleansed and freshened himself as well as he could;   3510
His face was bloodied and bruised
By the numerous hits he'd sustained,
So he washed his face before anything else;
Then he cleaned the blood from the place
On his body where the wound had occurred,   3515
But the wound made him fearful and worried,
Since clotting and bleeding continued on course
Because of the spearhead still lodged in his thigh.
With a powerful effort, he pulled it finally out,
Then cast about for something to bandage the wound,   3520
But all he find was a clump of moss,
Which he pulled from a dried-up tree;
It stung and was hard to apply,
But better by far than a mud-caked, malodorous thigh.

When he had given his wound a close look   3525
       And patched on the moss,
He took the spearhead he'd drawn out of his thigh
And concealed it in one of the ducts
That underground fed the fountain:
He wanted to keep it well out of sight.   3530
Once it was hidden, he stood up again,
Moving like the sore, hurting man that he was;
He went to lie down under the chapel.

God, how the maiden was weeping

As she watched at her window,   3535
Aware of the whole situation!
Her heart was stirred deeply
By all that she'd seen.
She'd seen the ambush by the thicket
And the men who leapt after Robert   3540
But failed then to catch him;
She'd seen him give back his arms
To the envoy in the half light of evening;
She'd seen his troublesome wound
And how he examined it closely   3545
And then dressed it with moss
And buried the spearhead he had pulled from his thigh.
The damsel was deeply upset
That he was so injured and woefully hurt.
As for the knight who had injured Robert,   3550
He was extremely distressed:
He believed in all truth he had lost God's trust
And that of the faithful.
He was long and deeply disturbed,
Blaming himself for the death   3555
(As he thought) of the valiant knight
Who'd defended the city with striking success.

"Rome's shown him her thanks
Like the dog close to drowning
Brought to the shore by a kindhearted swimmer: 3560
As soon as the creature is safely on land,
It shows no thanks for its rescue,
But barks at the man and is ready to bite.
I have behaved," he thought, "in a similar way.
Even worse am I than dirty old dogs."   3565

At that moment, his companions appeared;
They had caught up at last
And now asked what success he had had.

"My friends," he replied, "the news is dreadfully bad.

I intended to block the good knight's escape   3570
By killing his horse as he passed,
But I actually drove a long piece of my lance,
With the whole of the head, into his thigh.
Lord help me, I can't think what to do!
He has the head of my spear stuck in his flesh;   3575
The shaft, though, is out, all bloodied and splintered.
I am very upset and deeply disturbed,
For that man should have been not betrayed
But respected and honored,
With the great veneration we'd expect for a saint.   3580
True worth, alas, may win but a broken neck.
Such is the lesson we should never forget."

A t that, silence took hold;
     Every one of them felt a deep disappointment
That the good man had slipped from their grasp   3585
And that this had occurred on their watch!
Meanwhile, on shore, the Emperor
Felt such great joy in his heart
That his whole body throbbed with excitement:
The battle was over,   3590
The Saracens perished and gone!
He began to hand out the booty of war,
Dividing the gains with great fairness,
Except that he kept not a thing for himself,
Not even the worth of a single hen's egg.   3595
The noble man of high birth
Sent out a call for the precious white knight,
But no request or command
Brought any news of the man.
He appealed to the Pope, the Emperor did,   3600
And the bravest of all the young knights.
He invited them all,
With no distinction of rank,
As they were all worthy men,   3605
To join him that day in a great celebration,
A great feast at his table,

To honor their part in ending the war,
The barons didn't decline or seek an excuse;
They said right away   3610
They would gladly be there,
Since such was their Emperor's pleasure.
They betook themselves there with joy and delight,
Though with one major regret:
Not yet had they seen, nor yet had they met,   3615
Their defender and peerless protector.

"Have no fear," said the Emperor;
"If he left all the others
But passed near the thicket
Where I stationed quite a few of my men   3620
To catch him, they'll have caught him, I'm sure,
And will bring back their prize, safe and secure."

Just as they reached the end of that topic,
They saw come along the men of the ambush,
Looking downcast and wretched—a very sad sight.   3625
The Emperor rushed forward to meet them,
But then had to ask more than once
For news of what mattered the most.
He questioned them,
Eager to know   3630
Whether they'd caught the white knight,
The man more important than anyone else.

"My lord," they replied, "we don't have him.
We pursued him with all possible speed,
Not sparing ourselves for a moment;   3635
But only one of our number could reach him:
The knight you see here
With a blood-covered shaft in his hand.
He did manage to reach him, it's true,
And attempted to bring down his horse,   3640
But, just as misfortune

Overrules many a plan,
He happened to miss his true target;
As he was nearing the valley,
Almost abreast of the knight in white armor,   3645
No charm and no magic
Stopped him from striking his man in the thigh.
God grant the knight be healed of his wound,
For he is left with the head buried deep in his flesh!
Our companion is deeply distressed   3650
That he inflicted so grievous a hurt by pure chance;
You can see the blood-covered shaft of his lance!"

"He made a mistake," said the Emperor,
"But it was not a misdeed;
He is guilty of nothing beyond his control;   3655
Where his lance went he could hardly have known."

The Roman troops, hearing the news,
Knew it was no cause for rejoicing;
They all wept with bottomless grief.
The Emperor, too, melted into tears   3660
For the anguish he felt,
And he carried his sorrow back to the city.
Rome was now full of sad disappointment.
Women of every class and condition
Shed heartfelt, lingering tears   3665
For the man who had made such an effort
To save the people of Rome.

(Now he's departed, hurt and discouraged;
His good deed has become his great loss
And his deserts a source of dishonor.   3670
He helped us so much,
And what a reward he has had to accept!
What beautiful baggage he has carried away!
Ah, Rome, you horrible mob!
God should confound your whole town   3675
And make the ground sink under your feet!

You wrongfully killed
The valiant knight who saved you
From death and recalled you to life.
He enriched you   3680
With the treasure of Commenia,
Which now fills the coffers of Rome;
We owe it all to the man
Whom you have let vanish away
With a wound that is still gaping and grave.)   3685

Then they filed through the gate to the city,
All of them torn between sorrow and joy.
The Emperor proceeded
Toward the tapestried hall of the palace,
Leading the Pope   3690
And the noble barons of Rome.
They dismounted onto the time-honored perron
At the entrance to the hall
And handed their arms to the squires.
Then, once they had washed, they went in to dine.   3695
The powerful lords of the city
Took their seats at the tables;
Alongside that holy figure, the Pope,
Is where the Emperor took his place.
He called for the constable   3700
To escort the noble damsel, his daughter,
Who embodied for him all his joy;
He had her sit at his side
And bade her dine as he did,
Because nothing in the world did he love so much,   3705
And great love surpasses everything else.
Below, in the courtyard,
On the grass then in season,
Sat the most valorous fighters,
The noble of heart, those in love,   3710
The generous, and those of good breeding,
Who were glad to serve well and do honor,
The fine men of the petty noblesse,

Who are always a help in peace as in war.
Each one was served whatever he wanted;   3715
Food was abundant for all,
With a free flow of good wine through the feast;
Everyone had plenty to drink, plenty to eat.

R obert knew the time of the feast;
　 He would have preferred   3720
Not to take part this one time
As he normally would,
Because of his wound,
Which was troubling and painful;
But he had no excuse to be absent.   3725
His sole care was to do what he could
To avoid any hint, any sign
That might show any man who he was.
Weak and worried and visibly shaken,
Silently groaning, he entered the hall.   3730
He made his way slowly, with pain,
To the Emperor himself.
He hopped on one foot to make sure that the other
Could avoid touching the floor;
He steadied himself with a hand on his hip.   3735
When the fair, pale-white maiden espied him,
She rose from her seat in good greeting
Without even an instant's delay.
The elegant damsel, courteous and fine,
Bent low her beautiful head,   3740
Hands joined in modest respect,
Then courteously returned to her seat.
The Emperor was truly annoyed
To see her rise in greeting to a fool
Incapable of speech;   3745
He thought his lovely daughter no less a fool.
But when he saw his jester was limping,
He shook his head and muttered in anger,

"God!" he exclaimed, "what hateful people!

So vile and cruel, these Romans! 3750
God punish them!
I'd crush the skulls even of the best of them!
Their mad behavior has so distressed me
And done me such harm!
Why have they beaten my jester 3755
And injured him so badly
That his hip can only be dragged?
They've also torn and scarred
And bashed his face! Ah, God!
Look at the state they've left him in! 3760
In what bitter fights he was clearly abused,
To be so battered and bruised!"

After that moment, he muttered no more
But had a serving of food brought forth
And, before Robert's eyes, had it thrown to the dog; 3765
Robert seized no more, though,
Than just four little morsels,
Which he pulled from the dog only weakly;
And that effort he made only to hide
That it was more food than he could truly abide. 3770

T he Emperor was extremely displeased
To see that his jester was so badly hurt
That he barely glanced at his food.
The steward then ordered
The servants clear the cloths from the tables; 3775
He saw that the knights in attendance
Had had their fill of the feast
And wished to eat nothing more.
When the cloths were removed,
The knights and young men 3780
Traded talk of whatever they'd done,
Not wanting to hide—indeed, boasting about—
All their exploits of boldness and courage,
Yet not leaving out moments of fear and distress.
Such were the topics they all talked about, 3785

But one topic emerged as the favored by far:
The wondrous deeds of the knight in white armor!
Thanks to him, their side had defeated the Turks;
It was he who'd pursued them, he who had won;
It was he who had never relented   3790
Till the foe were all pushed to the port,
Then captured or drowned, slain and unmourned.

A t the table where were seated the counts,
   The Emperor discoursed at great length
About the knight who bore the white shield.   3795
In all the days of his life,
The Emperor declared,
No knight had ever fought so strikingly well;
Nor would there ever appear so peerless
A fighter, so valiant a man as he.   3800

"Three times has he rescued our city;
Three times has he saved our land;
Three times has he exalted the glory of Rome,
Without ever wanting it known
To any man born who he is.   3805
I don't know what he is—a king or an emperor?
A count or someone else of high birth?
Nowhere do I find a soul who might tell me;
But I know him to be a man of remarkable merit:
His concealment can be due to unique virtue alone,   3810
For I know of no other man in this land
Whose arms and whose efforts
Would have served us so well in our war;
No other man so richly deserving
A resounding reward would have failed   3815
To come forth with his claim.
This man, however, hides his face, stays away;
That is why I believe him of very high standing.
It pains me to think that he's injured.
If he appears, the wrong we have done him   3820
Will of course be redressed; he has but to agree!

Readily, without a moment's delay,
I will offer my daughter as his honorable wife.
No, he will have nothing to lose,
For, when I am gone, all Rome will be his;   3825
If he appears, he will be heir to it all,
Since he'll have wed my beautiful daughter."

The maiden, on hearing these words,
Pointed to the jester, pointed out the mute fool,
Showing her father as plainly as possible   3830
That it was the fool he was speaking about.
The Emperor dismissed her as foolish herself,
But the damsel refused to be stopped,
Showing him signs, signing her words,
Using her fingers to say   3835
That the jester deserved her father's great praise.

The Emperor was terribly puzzled.
He instructed his chamberlain
To send for the maiden's good ladies,
Determined to learn from them   3840
What his daughter wanted to say,
For now he saw her so out of control
As to feel unembarrassed
And fear no suggestion of shame.
The damsel's companions appeared,   3845
All governesses and servants as well,
And stood waiting for the word of the Emperor.
His daughter was filled with great apprehension.

"Ladies," the Emperor began,
"My daughter has shown me gestures and signs;   3850
I need to know what they mean."

The maiden, deeply offended
That she wasn't understood or believed
And her message not taken for true,
Once again made her gestures and signs   3855

To show that the jester was worthy
Of wearing the crown of the realm:
Was he not the most valiant man of them all?
The ladies, for whom the signs' meaning was clear,
Explained to the Emperor   3860
What his daughter wanted to say.

"My lord," said an old servant,
"Your daughter's tale
Is a childish invention, pure madness!
She claims, with greatest assurance,   3865
That that fool of a jester won the day's battle,
And she would readily swear
That he is the man you all prize,
For she saw all he was doing
From the window in her room;   3870
And in her language of signs she maintains
That she saw him armed in the morning,
Under the pine with the very broad branches,
With a suit of white armor and arms;
She watched as he left for the fight   3875
And, riding down past the thicket,
Then saw him rush into combat,
Striking the Turks and knocking them down;
She saw how he raced in pursuit,
Galloping all the way to the sea,   3880
And how he came back,
Riding through a great cloud of dust;
How he went past the thicket
Where an ambush was set in the shade of the trees;
How the knights leapt out   3885
But failed to detain him;
How one alone pushed ahead
And attempted to catch him
But only hit him in the thigh;
How he returned safe and sound   3890
Under the pine at the spring,
Where he painfully pulled out the lance

Whose head remained in the wound;
How he washed the wound of its blood,
Stanching the flow with some moss   3895
That he'd found in a dried-up old tree;
How he buried the head in the ground.
More than that, sire, she didn't tell us,
For she stopped her account at that point.
But she says she is hurt and ashamed   3900
That no one has deigned to believe her.
She knows not where to turn, except to the Lord,
To whom she incessantly prays
That he let her not go to her death
Before you have seen what she can't forget."   3905

"Good Lord!" the Emperor exclaimed.
"What a story! What nonsense!
What hermit, what cloistered old fool
Could have prompted so fantastic a tale?
It must have come from an all-seasons madman   3910
Who is so crazy and out of his mind
That his memory's gone along with his reason
And he has no idea of the arms in his hand
And has never uttered a word in his life!
So that's what appeals to my beautiful daughter,   3915
Obsessed as she is with that jester!
Neither of them is able to speak;
They behave like each other;
They share the same makeup and nature.
My daughter has turned all her thoughts   3920
To a mad, senseless love, and she thinks
There is nothing saner or more wise in the world."

"Ladies," the Emperor went on,
"I swear by the soul of my father
That, if you don't teach her more sensible ways,   3925
You shall soon taste
My displeasure and wrath
And I'll have you all put to imminent death!"

The servants were fearful as never before,
And the order frightened each governess, too;   3930
They escorted the damsel up to her rooms
And made every effort to care for her well.
Robert, meanwhile, hurt as he was,
Went down to his usual place
To find rest on his bed of fresh stubble,   3935
But his wound was painful and troubling.

The Emperor was in the great hall of the palace,
But there not to dance carols or rounds.
He summoned a council of barons
And proceeded with them to the chapel.   3940
There they held their discussion
And spoke at great length
Of the unknown white knight
Who so happily came to their aid
Though not asked for or summoned;   3945
The counselors discussed that at length.
The Emperor at the end did a summary
Of the various views they'd expressed.

"Lords," he said, "what can we do?
How can we find   3950
The wounded white knight?"

Said a counselor, "You can't ever find him
Without a ruse of some sort.
Swear right away, with no feint or deception,
You will allow him, should he wish,   3955
To take your gifted young daughter in marriage;
Then, when you die, the empire too shall be his,
For to no braver man or stronger defender
Could you bequeath it:
More resistant is he, more unyielding than iron.   3960
After taking your oath on the relics of saints,
Have this summons cried forth:
That all men of your land

Are to gather in outdoor assembly;
Through two days in a row, you too will attend   3965
And your daughter will likewise be present,
Wearing her imperial crown
For noble and powerful men to see and remember.
The man in white armor should join the assembly
And not be held back by any excuse   3970
But come with the others without any delay.
You will have him accept the dear maiden,
Provided he show the true proof of himself:
The head of the spear in his thigh and the wound.
By such a maneuver, by such clever means,   3975
You can succeed in finding the knight,
For no man from here as far as Compostela,
However grand or important,
If wedded to your beautiful daughter,
Would not be elated   3980
To encounter such outstanding success.
You will have granted him a handsome reward
If he'll now have both Rome and your daughter!"

The Emperor was pleased with this counsel,
And his barons, who heard it as well,   3985
Were equally pleased and indeed full of praise.
The Emperor swore and he pledged
That, if the knight were trusting enough
To appear at the palace,
He would go home happily wed, if he wished,   3990
To the Emperor's daughter!
So wise a proviso the father foresaw.

Then the crier was summoned,
That is, the one in charge of the corps;
He was given his orders and sent on his way.   3995
The meeting was over; the barons departed.
The criers went out to proclaim the announcement
That the Emperor had ordered.
This was accomplished with zeal, in good faith,

With no omission or feint. 4000
The news didn't take long
To spread through the land.
Men of all stations, rich and poor, clerics too,
Would show no hesitation
To show up at court 4005
To see an event of the most marvelous sort.

The seneschal, hearing word
Of the council and what it decided,
Didn't know what to say or to do.
He thought of this plan and that, 4010
Trying to imagine some scheme
That would allow him to claim the good damsel
Whom he loved most of all in the world.
His heart struggled with many an action.
He thought surely—in fact, had no doubt— 4015
That the knight equipped all in white
And reported to be so successful in battle
Would not come to claim his dear love;
Indeed, he had learned enough of his nature
To feel sure he was no creature of flesh and of blood 4020
And therefore posed no threat as a rival.
He thought now he'd adopt the other's appearance
And go in two days to the assembly in Rome;
Men and women would see him
All fitted out in white armor 4025
And with such equipment
As the white knight was said to have borne.
He knew how his disguise had to be,
For he had made all the needed inquiries
And asked questions and learned; 4030
It was the other he wished people to see.
Oh, but he would suffer many a trial
Before he could take the maiden to wife
Who was so remarkably gracious and lovely!
He maintained this decision, 4035
The fruit of considerable thought.

He had no time to spare;
He quickly ordered the making
Of a fresh white shield and handsome new arms,
White and precious and gleamingly new, 4040
Just like those borne by the knight
Who had saved and inspired the Romans.
Then he sought here and there, indeed everywhere,
Until he could find a proper white horse.
The steed was refreshed and well treated; 4045
It was given a harness just like the one
He'd been told had accoutered the mount
Used by the knight who'd made martyrs
Of the Turks in their cruel engagement.
Then he went off to a hidden spot 4050
All alone—now listen: it's true!—
On the day he was planning to leave,
And there did an astonishing thing
Whose like hadn't been seen ever before.
Hiding by himself in a corner, 4055
He set about committing so crazy an act
That no one could think it other than mad:
He took the long, sharp head of a spear
And pushed it into his thigh;
He hammered it in with a mallet, 4060
Which caused him horrible pain;
Then he carefully, tightly, tied up the wound
So the spear head would stay where it was.
May God let him not heal,
Because he wanted the credit for another man's deed! 4065
Once that was done,
He took his white weapons
Into an orchard and there, under branches,
Armed himself calmly, in hiding,
Since he had no wish to be seen. 4070
When he was armed in well-equipped splendor
And far from the eyes of anyone watching,
He mounted, with effort and pain, on his horse.
Now he was ready for his life's greatest folly.

He hung his white shield 'round his neck;   4075
He rode away all alone, with no waiting at all
And moved with all speed to Rome,
Where the Emperor and all of his men
Were gathered in a major assembly.
From everywhere in the land had they come—   4080
Counts and dukes, princes and barons
(Who hardly arrived unattended),
And vavasors of illustrious birth;
Never had anyone seen so superb an assembly!
The Pope himself was present as well,   4085
The glorious Pope, the most saintly;
He had also convoked all the clergy
To enhance even further this unusual meeting;
There were abbots and monks,
Consecrated priests, clerks, and canons,   4090
Bishops, archbishops, and hermits
And the holy recluse who lived
In the forest far away from the crowd—
The man who, it happens, was Robert's confessor!
He had received the Pope's word of the council   4095
And a papal command that he come
To pray with them all
That God might soon send the white knight;
The recluse was told to be present,
Letting no other task hold him back.   4100
He was given a place at the side of the Pope,
There to voice everyone's longing and hope.

The Emperor, the story now tells us,
    Sat on an ivory stool,
Beside him his beautiful daughter,   4105
Whom the father treated not ill,
But with a very lover's attention.
He had placed on her head
A coronet of bright gold.
The maiden was lovely,   4110
Charming and bright and adorably simple,

Lips and cheeks more red than a rose,
Throat more lovely and white than a lily;
She was truly a joy to behold!
She was splendidly dressed   4115
In brown delicate silk studded
With flecks of fine gold.
The people were already assembled;
All day they'd been waiting in place
And no one by nones had yet moved.   4120
Now they were moved by the fear,
The terrible thought, that surely somehow
They had missed the knight armed in white.
They were all disappointed, more and more certain
That he wouldn't come to the council   4125
And would never be heir to the crown.

As the Romans were feeling their fear,
Just as they were worrying most,
The seneschal came through the gate,
All alone, with no groom in attendance.   4130
Holding his gleaming white lance in his hand,
He was alone as he rode, moved forward alone,
As his white banner fluttered down
To the side bars of his saddle;
And he had at his neck a gleaming white shield   4135
That was long and heavy and broad.
Fully armed and astride his white steed,
He rode down through the streets.
As soon as he was spotted
And seen within Rome,   4140
People appeared at windows and doorways
And thresholds to watch
As he passed on his way,
And they sent up acclamations of joy
So great that the noise of their pleasure   4145
Resounded through the whole of the city.
Children and ladies and maidens,
Servant girls and young damsels,

City dwellers and craftsmen,
Courtiers and peasants   4150
Came running and shouting their greetings
Before him and rolling out through the streets
Mats and carpets and quilts,
And everyone bowed with hands clasped in welcome.
As soon as he entered the main street in the center,   4155
The crowd pressed around him;
The commotion in Rome,
The carryings-on of both women and men
Were so stunningly loud and unruly
That the Emperor, listening,   4160
Was not sure what to do,
Stupefied as he was by all the confusion.
Others present were just as nonplussed
By the turmoil of the enormous event.
News didn't stop going around,   4165
And people ran to the council
That the Emperor was holding at court.

Everyone cried, "He is coming, he's coming!
The white knight is now on his way!
He's joining the crowd! We've seen him!"   4170

Oh, had you witnessed all those people excited,
Noblemen weeping and shaking,
Deeply moved, overcome with elation!
Everyone threw up his hands to the Lord
And gave him the honor of heartfelt thanks.   4175
The Emperor, for his part,
Glowed with all the same joy.
His daughter, however, shook her blond locks
And showed no such delight.
Her face was pale, and her body was trembling;   4180
She feared a trick and a dreadful event,
For she well knew it was all a great lie,
Knew that this wasn't the knight
Whom the people were all acclaiming so loudly,

The knight who had fought the rude battle.   4185
He, she knew, lay under the chapel,
Sorely wounded, in tatters, unshod.
The seneschal arrived at that point,
And clearly enough for no one to miss him.
The crowd exploded with joy   4190
The moment they saw him appear;
There was no holding back all the tears
Of emotion that sprang from their hearts,
For his coming was a deeply wished-for event;
Had they seen our Lord,   4195
They'd have felt no greater reward.

T he Emperor could not have been more exultant;
    It was as if he were holding God by the feet!
The knights, however, were somewhat surprised,
And a number exchanged their impressions   4200
That this man, after all,
Did not truly resemble
The white knight they had seen,
Whose great efforts had vanquished the Turks—
No, they simply did not resemble each other!   4205

"Look," they said, "have you ever seen
So sorry a figure, so small and unimposing?"

And the closer he came,
The more he seemed to them out of place;
Many observers were doubtful,   4210
Though most rejected their view
And maintained that nothing was wrong:

"That's the effect of his wound, which is painful
And makes him look stooped and bent over."

Words flew back and forth and grew louder;   4215
The Emperor found them disturbing
And wanted the buzzing to cease.

He sent the town crier to the roof of the palace
To have him announce that
Further word was not to be said   4220
And all were to stay at their places
And not move anywhere else;
They must remain peaceful and quiet
If they valued their safety!
With that, the disputing was over   4225
And the disturbance came to an end.
The seneschal then came forward,
Visibly pained, like a man who'd been injured.
The barons, to a man, rose to show their respect
And bowed low and long;   4230
None, though, moved from his seat,
Save the few who ran to the seneschal's
Stirrups to help him dismount;
He waited a long moment, however,
Before starting down to the ground;   4235
He asked to be aided with careful attention,
As his wound of course caused him considerable pain.
What he wished was then done;
Softly and gently
They lifted him deferentially down,   4240
Several men helping to hold him,
Since he couldn't stand on both feet;
Only one foot could he put on the ground.
With evident pain, he made his way to the Emperor
To claim the prize he deemed promised.   4245
His helmet, shining bright as a mirror,
Was now unlaced and removed,
Since the man felt so close to his goal;
He just retained on his head the white lining,
Which was whiter than snow new fallen on pine.   4250

I n a loud and sharp voice
He spoke: "Just Emperor," he said,
"I have come to your court,
From which I long stayed away,

Not for any litigious purpose,   4255
But because it is proper I be here.
It is I who have fought in your service
And merited the gift
Of your daughter and land.
I have come here to make my claim known.   4260
Grant it me with no untoward delay
And consider there is no time to wait,
For I plan to turn home very soon.
Have your daughter make ready!
I have won her by arms in true battle   4265
And shall now wed her in church."

The Emperor replied, "You shall have her,
But first we must see the place
Of your wound and the injury itself,
As well as the spearhead—all signs of the truth.   4270
Whatever you are—Breton, French, or whatever—
You shall not have my daughter
Without revealing such proofs
Before all these witnesses present."

"My lord," he responded, "I ask nothing less!   4275
If I am unable to furnish such proof,
Then it is right that my claim be denied."

Then he asked to be gripped and held tight
So not to fall, then bared his thigh
And with both hands opened his wound;   4280
With strain and pain and great effort
He pulled the blade from his leg
And presented it then to the Emperor,
All the while making a show
Of the terrible toll that the extraction was taking.   4285
The barons who were watching his show
Felt his pain as if it were theirs;
They were shocked by his wound
When they saw how black and ugly it was.

"This is no laughing matter,"   4290
They all said, young and old;
"This man merits our trust and our honor."

Then the Emperor attested
That no doubt could remain
That this was the man of whom it was said   4295
That he caused the pagans such terrible shame.
There could now be no greater joy!
Still, even better to know
The whole truth of what happened,
He called on the knight   4300
Who had wounded the hero:
Let him come forth without fear,
And his act will of course be forgiven
Once the Emperor's new son has been crowned!
But fear made the knight tremble   4305
As he walked up to the Emperor,
Who gave him the spearhead to inspect,
A blade very sharp, very cutting.

"Friend," said the Emperor, "consider this weapon
And be sure, on your life,   4310
That you not tell me a lie,
For then you would face a sure death.
I want you to tell me in truth
Whether this blade came from your lance,
The very same spear that you used   4315
When you took aim at our knight
And hit him right in his thigh."

Alas, the young fellow knew not what to say,
For he saw that the blade was unfamiliar to him.
Still, whether for good or for ill,   4320
Was he not bound to tell the truth as he knew it?
His heart felt tugged in every direction,
Since he knew with no doubt
That the blade had not come from his lance:

He would certainly spot his own blade 4325
If he saw it—there was simply no question—
And this spearhead was surely not his.
What to do? What to say?
If he decided to state the blade was not his,
No one would believe what he said, 4330
And they'd all cry, "It's a lie!"
But if he really lied and called it the truth,
He'd be guilty of betraying his lord.
The knight was bewildered
And turned to God for his guidance. 4335
He then made the best choice he could see
And entertained no further thought:
He would acknowledge the blade as his own!
He would no doubt receive a rich gift
—A reward—from the knight 4340
Who was seeking the hand of the damsel
And would welcome this end to his suit.
The seneschal told him
He was taking too long:
Let him say if the blade was indeed from his lance! 4345
Had he not examined it long enough?
Let him end this excessive delay
And, before all observers, he would now be forgiven
The wound his poor aim and impatience had caused!
The young knight bowed low and uttered his thanks. 4350
Then he turned to the Emperor and said,

"My lord, have no hesitation;
There is no doubt concerning this man.
He fought to protect all your people
And he defended your land; 4355
He is the man who safeguarded your honor,
As this is surely my spearhead
That he drew from his thigh,
The blade I had used to do him great harm.
He has earned his reward." 4360

"He shall have his reward," said the Emperor,
"My beautiful, noble young daughter!
I will see to their marriage, of course,
And will also, before they depart,
Grant him to inherit my crown."   4365

Then he turned to the man
To acknowledge his standing
Before all the barons.
Hear now the seneschal's devilish terms
Once he'd heard the Emperor's generous words: 4370

"Dear good sir," said the Emperor,
    "You who wish to possess the empire
And the lordship of Rome,
I wish to know basic facts of your life.
Do not keep from me who you are   4375
And the name that you bear.
There is much that I wish to know about you,
Where you are from and the land of your birth.
You have done me remarkable service
By slaying my foes in such numbers."   4380

The seneschal then offered his answer
In the following words:

"My lord, I am no stranger to you
And I know not how to pander or flatter.
For a long while I served you   4385
And did much to earn your affection.
I am in fact your own seneschal,
He who has now restored all the losses
And mended the damage inflicted on Rome.
My lord, if you were ever cruel toward me or unfair,   4390
Know that I have never let it sap my allegiance."

The Emperor looked at him then
And understood who he was.

He remembered his delicate face,
Bright and ruddy and fresh.   4395

"What, seneschal," said the Emperor,
"Is that you?"

"It is indeed, my lord."

"God!" the Emperor replied,
"Who's ever heard so wondrous a tale!
Now I am sure that God is my guide,   4400
Enhancing my power and bringing me honor."

At these words, he ran up to the man
Without uttering an additional sound
And held him fast in a tight embrace;
He gave him a hundred fast kisses,   4405

And "God!" he said, "what relief I now feel!
What more can I ever lament,
Since I now have all I could want?
This man, who opposed me so fiercely,
Has thrice come to rescue my land   4410
And fight on my side.
He went to war in a place
Where, had anyone known him,
He would not have escaped
Being slain in great pain.   4415
But now our Lord God has willed
That he should be the master in Rome.
Before now my men tried
To speak in his favor;
They often attempted to soften my heart,   4420
But cruel harshness
Would never allow me
To grant him in marriage
My dear-hearted, beautiful daughter.
Now, though, I have vowed this to God: 4425

The people of Rome shall have him
As their living protector. I will it so!
And I shall be true to my word.
He shall have all that God has prescribed:
Empire and crown—and my daughter, my pride!"   4430

When the seneschal heard this,
    He was so overjoyed
That he threw himself at the feet of the Emperor,
Who, however, immediately raised him
And led him up to the maiden.   4435
She, for her part, was grievously shocked
And came close to bursting with rage.
In her heart and her thoughts she besought
Our Lord to offer her guidance
And send her the means   4440
To reveal the seneschal's
Trick, the dastardly ruse
Whereby he sought to mislead everyone.
She prayed she might die
And that sudden death overcome her   4445
Before she were his and held tight in his power.

"My lady," questioned the counts,
"Why do you weep? Have you no shame?
Such behavior is not proper or bright!
This is a time for great joy,   4450
When a valiant man of such standing deigns
To sue for your love as his wife.
You should be grateful to God,
Yet instead you do nothing but weep!"

When those in the crowd now assembled   4455
Heard the report
That the knight who had helped them so much
In their defense
Was no man but their own seneschal
Now come to claim the empire as his,   4460

There was such an outburst of joy
That God's thunder itself could hardly be heard.
The Emperor came up to his daughter,
Holding the man by his hand.

"Daughter," he said, "rejoice   4465
And show a courteous, well-mannered welcome,
For I bring you your spouse!
I give your husband to you
And you to him in proper marriage.
Welcome him now with a grateful heart.   4470
He is the seneschal of my land,
Who for you had warred against me,
But he is the bold and valiant knight,
Brave and ready to fight,
The strong, handsome, white-shielded man   4475
Thanks to whom we have gained a new life.
He rescued us; he it was who made us safe once again.
The Turks, thanks to him, were defeated.
He was for us three times in a row
So effective a fighter, so fine a defender,   4480
That the Turks could not hurt us
Or shame us, do us harm, or defeat us
But fled instead in a fearsome rout.
Daughter, offer him now a most gracious greeting;
Welcome him with no further delay   4485
And put an end to your tears.
Let it be clear to God the Most High
That this is the very same knight
Who performed such wonders in battle!"

"Dear father," ventured the maiden,   4490
"He is not the right man!"

"Daughter, he exclaimed, "Is it you that I hear?
Can it truly be you, speaking like that?
You, who have started to speak?"

"My dear good father," said the maiden,   4495
"Yes, I have been mute all these years
Till this day, till this hour,
When you took me by surprise
With your wish that I take the seneschal
And make him my spouse.   4500
God does not want me to have him,
For he is not a man
Who was wounded in battle.
Everything he has told you is pure fabrication,
As I am not the only person to know.   4505
Very close to where we stand is the man
Who vanquished and crushed all the Turks
And in the end paid a quite heavy price,
For he was injured and maimed in the fight.
God, sorely angered by all that occurred,   4510
Has for that reason performed a miraculous feat
Which will be remembered forever,
For he has now made me able to speak."

When her father heard her speak,
He ran forward with kisses of joy.   4515
I doubt we'll ever again be able to see
Such wonderful joy in a single embrace!
No one present failed to feel all that joy
Without being moved at the same time to tears.
The news of rejoicing ran through the court   4520
As throngs and as crowds
Pressed through the palace
To witness the miraculous feat
And hear the young damsel finally speak.

The seneschal took it in truth to mean   4525
That God wished him confounded;
This was to be the misfortune he earned
By attempting to fool and betray his good lord.
While the crowd was growing thick
And people jostled one another,   4530

And all were trying to force themselves forward,
So that no one paying him heed,
The seneschal felt free not to tarry.
He turned around through the crowd
Like a traitorous, criminal schemer;   4535
He went fleeing toward his horse,
With no one attempting to stop him;
Nor did he think of the pain in his leg,
His injury or wound.
He was wholly unnerved by what he was seeing.   4540
He ran to his mount
And gripping the stirrups, leapt into the saddle;
He fled at high speed,
Bearing the onus
Of misfortune and shame,   4545
Which to this day has clung to his name.

Now I shall tell you what women and men
Were doing in the crowd assembled in Rome.
They were so joyful and happy,
As I see in my source,   4550
That they thought themselves free of sadness forever.
The brightest of the barons, the most worldly,
Flocked to the maiden and gathered around.
The miraculous, beautiful wonder
Made them weep with joy and remarkable gladness.   4555
The Emperor, in tones noble and grave,
And in tears, addressed these words to his daughter
As he took her in his arms:

"Daughter," he said, "I am greatly relieved
But astonished as well   4560
By what I have heard you declare—
That you know to be here among us the savior
Worthy of possessing this land,
The man who brought our wars to an end.
You apparently know something true about him;   4565
Tell us, if you can,

Where we can find him.
Never can we hear any word about him
That would place your marriage in doubt
Or stop him from inheriting this imperial house." 4570

"Father," responded the damsel,
"I can readily give you news
Of the noble good knight,
Who has been ten long years in this city,
Though no one has acknowledged or known him 4575
Or been able to learn his true name,
Whatever the terms to which he responds.
Now God wishes no longer to hide him
But wants to use me to raise him on high;
God grants me the honor of making him known. 4580
It is for the good knight himself,
Glorious and holy as he is,
Who three times saved the city of Rome,
That God gave me the gift of my power of speech;
It is for him he performed such a wonder. 4585
He lies down below,
Under the vault of the chapel.
He is the man we have called our fool,
Who always eats with the dog.
I tell you he is no fool, no jester or madman, 4590
But a valorous, sensitive knight
Of the most noble origin and birth;
Both mother and father came from the highest of ranks.
An act of penance has made him conceal it
In the ways and the manner 4595
That you have seen through the years.
Many times you have blamed me
And taken me to task
For showing you signs
That he was worthy of respect and of honor 4600
And it was he that people had on their minds
And that everyone was praising so highly;
But you never wished to believe me,

Insisting instead that my signs were untrue,
Mere inventions and folly,   4605
A joke born of fatigued melancholy;
You even had me removed from the table.
Father, God now wants to confirm
The statement I was making
About the knight I esteem,   4610
Who is lying unshod and untended under the stairs.
Where is the seneschal now?
It seems he's become newly mute.
People all say he took flight,
Lest the crowd seize him and strike."   4615

When this news reached the ears
Of the Emperor and high barons
And they saw they'd lost track of the trickster
Who had approached them with lies and deceit,
They were grieved to know he'd escaped—   4620
Elated, however, by the other event
That the maiden recounted:
The news that the man they had taken for mad
And had treated with superb disregard
Was in truth the valiant knight   4625
Who had undone the whole Turkish force.
What a wonder that was! How amazing!
The depth of the feeling it caused
Brought tears to the eyes of everyone present.

"Good Lord," they exclaimed, "what a tale!   4630
Where else in the world has there ever been word—
Where else has such news been reported or heard
As the wondrous event we have witnessed right here?
Lord God," they went on, "grant us mercy!
Whoever denies you is an ignorant peasant!   4635
We thought till a moment ago
That that man was a fool and a dumb featherbrain
And now we learn he came fighting for us
And fought so remarkably well and so bravely

That all by himself   4640
He won the whole battle
And destroyed those perfidious Turks!"

"Lords," said the damsel,
    "There is more I must tell you,
And you will surely believe me,   4645
As I have positive proof to provide.
I do not find the man very bright
Who just now held the lance head
That the seneschal showed;
It brought you some great reassurance   4650
But its true value was nil!
He maintained that the blade was his own
And that he inflicted the wound near the wood
On that fellow who deserves no favor of God.
He fed you a bald-faced lie!   4655
It was all fake, from bulla and seal
To every word of his claim.
I know quite well where the blade is located,
Because I saw it stowed there in hiding
By the knight who wished no one to find it.   4660
No longer at this point can I help keep his secret,
But must say what I know—clearly speak it!"

The maiden, who was comely and noble,
    Was neither languid nor slow,
Not gross or a fool or dim-witted;   4665
She unclasped her cloak
And, robe-less, with greatest simplicity,
Walked out through the crowd
And into the garden, where she went to the fountain;
Under the grass near the sand pit   4670
She unearthed the spearhead secreted in the ground;
No need had there been to search very long!
With that, she returned to her father,
Lighthearted and joyful, with a radiant smile,
And handed him the blade of the lance.   4675

The many important men who were present
Watched as he took it to hold and examine;
He commanded right away
That the knight make haste to come forward
To whom the blade was said to belong.   4680
He handed him the object and warned
That he give no thought to a lie
But say if indeed he was the owner
Of that fine, solid weapon.
At the sight of the blade, the knight felt afraid   4685
And fell to the feet of the Emperor.

"My lord," he said, "I swear by our living God,
I brought this blade from Pavia,
Where it was made and I bought it.
There is no finer of its kind from here to Caesarea;   4690
This summer I have had it in my keeping
Seven years and more,
And it's with this weapon that I stabbed the man
Whose fate so concerns the people of Rome
And causes such worry."   4695

Companions made haste to confirm the knight's story.

"K night, the Emperor replied,
"Tell me now, by the soul of your father,
Why you lied when you earlier spoke
Of the weapon you had in your hand."   4700

"My lord," said the knight, "I shall tell you,
And no word will be an untruth.
I saw the seneschal standing before you
With your whole heart inclined in his favor
And everyone else convinced of his honor   4705
And wishing him well and every success
As he soon took his dear love as his wife.
I understood that the marriage, my lord,
Could hardly take place

If I ventured to deny the tale of the blade   4710
(And leave myself open to everyone's hate).
If I have betrayed you in this,
Please understand and forgive;
No second offense shall there be as long as I live!"

The Emperor declared the man pardoned   4715
When the daughter he so loved
Sweetly made that request;
He readily granted her wish
Because of his joy at the wondrous event.
He was now impatient to see   4720
The man who lay wounded under the chapel.
He summoned ten of his principal barons
—The best he could choose—
To a conciliar meeting.

"Lords," he began, "here is your task,   4725
And be sure not to tarry:
Bring me the knight
Whom you will find downstairs in the crypt;
We must hear what he'll say."

No one dared to oppose such an order.   4730
They went to look for the knight
Downstairs under the vault;
There the injured man lay
Face drained of all color and drawn;
They found him sighing and moaning;   4735
They bade him sit up
And Robert made no attempt to refuse,
But painfully, slowly, he rose and moved forward
And did whatever they asked.
He knew not what they wanted or meant,   4740
Hurting and dazed as he was.
They raised him by the pits of his arms
And in their arms forced him forward,
Away from the spot he had known as his own.

He was suffering so much from his wound,   4745
—That man who was chivalry itself—
That his anguished laments were readily heard
And he indeed felt close to his death.
But those who had borne him upstairs
Now brought him into the council   4750
Right up to the Emperor of Rome
And the Pope and the old holy hermit
And various others who were present as well.
They all greeted him with greatest rejoicing!
They rose to their feet in respect,   4755
Careful not to touch or otherwise hurt him.
The beautiful damsel was there in the crowd
But was the first to step forward and bow.

O n a seat of solid gold
    Was Robert told to be seated,   4760
Looking straight at the Emperor.
Now he was terribly fearful
Lest all he had done become known;
Very much, my source tells me,
Did he want to keep it all hidden.   4765
The Romans were so moved as they watched him
That the honor they offered
Was mixed with the tenderest tears
For his pain and obvious torment.
As soon as the clamor had calmed,   4770
The Emperor spoke these encouraging words:

"Good man," he said, "my brother and friend,
Tell me please who you are.
By what name shall I call you?
We have now learned your secret   4775
And seen your loyal and remarkable work;
We see how you choose to behave
And understand why you have hidden from us:
A penitent is no doubt what you are.
Understand we intend no offense   4780

If we seek to know who you are.
In God's name, we exhort you
To put an end to concealment
And let your real story now be revealed!"

Robert made no attempt to speak for himself;   4785
His eyes filled with tears, his heart with deep sighs;
He was stunned by the crowd awaiting his answer,
Realizing too well he'd been sorely betrayed.

"Knight," said the maiden,
"I too was long mute,   4790
Unable to speak till today.
Now love for you has led God in his kindness
To grant me the power of speech;
This occurred just after noon.
God wants you crowned lord   4795
Of the land and master of the empire.
I beseech you in his name
To tell us your story—
Who you are and whence you arrived
When you chose to dwell here and to hide."   4800

Robert offered no word in reply,
However much the maiden insisted;
He could respond only with tears of deep feeling
That thanked our Lord he had granted the damsel
The power of speech and allowed her to speak   4805
The very words he had just heard her utter.
When the gentle young lady saw
There was no way she could draw
Even a word from the tearful young knight,
She too shed tenderest tears.   4810
She appealed to the Pope, saying,

"Sir, for the sake of the Lord, Creator of the world,
Do please entreat him to speak, if only to you,
Since to us he denies any hearing:

Our pleas have had no success."   4815

The Pope turned to Robert:

"Brother," he said, "please don't be upset
By what I am going to say.
I beseech you, in the name of our glorious God,
To recount what you can of your life   4820
Before you came here.
It would be a great kindness."

Robert said not a word, but remained very still;
What he heard did not please him at all.
When the Pope saw that the man   4825
Still refused to explain what was asked,
He knew not where to turn
To learn what he could about the man's life
If not to the hermit, the holy old man
Who normally lived in the depths of the forest.   4830
He gently asked for his help,
And the hermit was kind to agree.
He addressed the young knight
Who had once been a guest in his house:

"Friend," said the hermit,   4835
"In the name of our God, I ask you to say
Who you are. I need to know,
Should you wish, through me,
To find grace and God's blessing."

Robert felt no fear at these words,   4840
But instead was both pleased and relieved,
For until now he had had to make painful efforts
Not to yield to such pleading.
Now, before the holy hermit, all pretense was gone.

"Sir," he replied, "I shall tell you   4845
And not lie in the slightest.

Since you exhort me to speak,
I shall tell you the truth
About all that you ask.
I will not keep my secret from you,   4850
But tell you the truth, as is right that I do.
Sir, Normandy is where I was born;
The man who was Duke was my father,
And the Duchess, my mother.
The Count of Poitiers, good sir,   4855
Was, I tell you, my forebear.
I was born, though, in a way defiant of nature:
My mother, by mischance,
Asked that the Devil beget me.
By his command I grew to commit   4860
Wicked deeds in my deplorable youth,
For which here, as you've seen,
I have done a long penance.
Now I have told you the gist of my tale
And tell you as well, without shame: 4865
'Robert' was I baptized; 'Robert' is my name."

At the assembly were present
Four gray-haired barons of evident age—
Important knights of Normandy.
They had been a long while in Rome,   4870
Hoping to learn whatever they could,
Whatever good news, of Robert, their lord,
Whom they had sought through many a land,
Undeterred by whatever hindrance or war.
The statement they heard Robert make   4875
Was a wonder of joy and relief.
All four, as they stood and facing the crowd,
Rushed forward to fall at his feet.
Tears flowed from their eyes
As they cried for his mercy and shouted their thanks.   4880

"Noble lord," the barons exclaimed,
"Your vassals implore you—have mercy!

They are being attacked from all over.
In God's name, come to their rescue!
Lord, do not delay   4885
Or be dissuaded by love male or female.
Come to the aid of your people,
Who are wrongfully threatened
By forces of your very own clan.
Every day they bring harm and destruction   4890
To the people of your land,
All ravaged by continual war.
Lord, the Duke, your father, is dead
And so is the Duchess, your mother.
So, too, is the powerful Count, your grandfather,   4895
Who so loved those dearest to him.
Now are their fiefs all in your possession.
No man, my lord, is worthy of them,
Except you, and yours they must be!
Your cousins, however, aim to betray you   4900
And want to steal what is yours.
Let them not dispossess you!
Lord, you have already waited too long."

When the Emperor heard
Robert and his barons and the whole of their story,   4905
He was overjoyed as never before;
The news brought by the Normans
Gave Robert so high a rank and such importance,
Such power and so prestigious a family,
That the Emperor felt more joy in his heart   4910
Than he could ever have hoped to feel.
He came up to Robert, in full view
Of all the people assembled,
And gently spoke in these terms:

"Robert, my friend," said the Emperor,   4915
"If the Duke, your father, is dead,
A man of such valor in life,
Be not troubled and feel not bereft,

For I shall be a true father to you;
You shall have my daughter as wife,   4920
And I will bequeath my empire to you.
I want you to be lord, to be master,
Chief and commander,
Justicer and, yes, even Emperor."

"Emperor," exclaimed the Normans,   4925
"We could hardly consider it wise,
If, to take your daughter in marriage,
He abandoned the defense of his land,
Which can only remain ravaged and waste
If he fails to go save it in haste."   4930

Robert then spoke, "Lords, hear me!
I ask you, in God's name, to be calm.
Turn back to your land,
For I am one who will never again
Belong to this world as long as I live.   4935
I will instead keep close watch on my soul,
Lest the Enemy try to surprise me
And make me attend to that which is empty and vain.
I wish not to lose my place in God's Heaven.
You have heard description enough   4940
Of the man that I was and the ill that I did;
I will not leave here to fall back into evil.
Look among the members of my family
For a worthy and wise and valiant man
Who could take control of my fief;   4945
Such is the man you must find.
I give you this order with no further discussion;
This is my firm and final decision."

"Good friend," the Emperor then said,
"Accept the gift I just promised;   4950
It comes from the heart."

"Lord," exclaimed Robert, "I can't and I won't!

Never, please God, son of Mary,
Will I risk the loss of my soul,
This soul I have made every effort to save!   4955
All you possess
I reject, along with your beautiful daughter.
Never, please God, will she be
Deflowered by me,
Nor caressed or embraced.   4960
No pleasure will I seek
As long as my soul remains in this body.
I shall instead go away with the hermit
Who abides in the great lonely forest
And whom I shall never abandon.   4965
Together with him, I shall serve the Martyr
Who for our sake suffered torment
And by his death confounded the Devil.
One favor I ask of your kindness:
That in view of my service to you   4970
You have me borne to the forest
Where the hermitage stands,
Where I want my wound to be healed
And through mortification purify my flesh:
That is the goal and the end of my striving.   4975
I have become too attached to the hermit
Ever to wish myself elsewhere;
I choose to live by his side.
Since you now know my whole story,
I am ready to leave, not stay here any more.   4980
Were I to be offered the whole of the earth,
With all that it holds all about,
With all that its people everywhere have
And all of the wealth it contains,
I would still not postpone my departure   4985
Or stay one more day in this world.
Now I ask you, please,
To bear me away from this place,
For my injury gives me great pain;
I must go to the forest, there to remain."   4990

The Emperor then answered,
"Since neither my land nor my silver or gold
Can make you remain here in Rome,
I shall let you be carried off to the home
Of the hermit who is sitting right here.   4995
But no man is there here who is not sorrowed
—Indeed, deeply pained—
To see you depart from our midst."

Said the hermit, "Lord Emperor,
Now that Robert has chosen for father   5000
Our heavenly God and almighty King,
And will be a hermit alongside of me,
Let him depart as I do;
You cannot keep him
Once he has given himself to Christ our Lord.   5005
He wants no further harassment
By Foe, Fiend, or Devil,
But rather wants his heart firmly fixed
In the service of our Lord Jesus Christ,
Who created the world and conceived Paradise."   5010

The Emperor responded, "There is no more to say.
Since nothing and no one can stop him,
I shall of course have a litter bear him away."

He then summoned his workmen
And had them fashion a litter,   5015
Fit it out and made ready;
They laid Robert comfortably down,
And that was the end of his long years in Rome.
Boys and ladies and maidens,
Young girls, damsels, and lads,   5020
The Emperor, his barons, and men
Followed the litter
A long league from the city.
Everyone was sad-faced and tearful
When they bade Robert farewell   5025

And commended him to the grace of our Lord.
Then the hermit, who shared his longing for God,
Led him on, a forest away from all that he was.

Robert was healed and recovered his strength,
And before long the time came   5030
When the saintly hermit in his sleep passed away,
He whom God showed that he cherished
The pains he had suffered for him.
I have no doubt he earned his reward.
Indoors in the hermit's own chapel,   5035
That most holy of men was interred
While Robert lay plunged into grief.

Here our story relates
That Robert survived a long time,
Serving God with earnest devotion   5040
In the place of the hermit.
For his sake, God performed many wonders
In this world here below when he still lived,
Even before his life ended,
So that people who came for his help   5045
Had no doubt he was saintly himself.

At the end, he died in his forest,
Where the hermitage had remained his true home.
The people of Rome, when word reached them,
Came as quickly as they possibly could;   5050
In a display of intense and heartfelt devotion,
They came in a lengthy and stirring procession.
They removed his remains from the chapel
And bore Robert's body to Rome.
He was interred there at the church   5055
Called Saint John Lateran,
Where in the tomb to the right as you enter
He was buried midst a throng of clerics and priests.
The tomb is still there; there it is found
And there it remains—   5060

At least insofar as I've heard.
There was then a great conclave in Rome,
With people attending from many a land,
To make peace after too many wars.
One of the men in attendance   5065
Was a powerful lord from Le Puy.
He inquired into the life of Saint Robert,
Then stole from his tomb
The bones that he found there
And returned to his country.   5070
Near Le Puy, on the bank of a river,
In the name of Robert, brought back from Rome,
He founded an abbey, rich and impressive.
He gave it an abbot, with monks and with priests—   5075
And a glorious creation it was!
The splendid abbey still stands there,
Known to us all as Saint Robert.

NOTES

Lines 341–42. This passage in French is awkwardly phrased, suggesting that Robert is aided in his vicious attack by armed culprits. Context makes the matter clear: nowhere in this whole episode or its aftermath is there any allusion to persons aiding Robert in the mayhem. It appears that lines 341 and 342 were transposed in the manuscript, giving a false impression that the barons and retainers were companions of Robert rather than associates of the convent.

Lines 1080–86. The incident involving a "lightening" of the meal may refer to a *trou normand* filled with (cervine) bone marrow. True, that would be a very peculiar palate cleanser or even noncleansing appetite stimulant—but medieval ideas of gastronomy are often different from ours. Besides, the reference *might* be meant ironically. Compare the note in Gaucher's edition of version B (*Robert le Diable: Édition bilingue*, lines 1348–52, page 165, note 88).

Lines 2169–70. The original lines are literally "arms more white than snow on the branches." Compare lines 402–3, 427, and 1793–95, where *une arme blanche* is as unproblematic in modern French as it is in Old French, for the term "white arms" consistently denotes cutting-and-thrusting weapons, generally silver in color. In English the comparison here requires a shift from "snow" to "ice" and a descriptive word such as "gleaming" in the place of an adjective of color. Elsewhere, with no such comparison in the immediate context, a literal rendering of "white" is acceptable, especially because of its common association with purity.

Lines 2289–91a. The manuscript (version A) shows a lacuna at this point, as does the manuscript transmitting the later redaction (version B, edited by Gaucher in *Robert le Diable: Édition bilingue*, at page 217). The interpolation posited here is suggested by Gaucher (ibid.). Gaucher's hypothesis is surely correct (as opposed to Micha's, which fails to recognize that the topic has turned back from the girl to the unknown knight). My adaptation of her interpretation requires the insertion of an extra line, 2291a. See lines 3779–87 for a similar scene, one readily serving as model for the interpolation.

Line 2343. Mamistra (also Mopsuestia, later Misis, in Turkey) was the site of an important battle in 1152 between the Armenians of Cilicia and the forces of the Byzantine Empire; the Armenians were victorious.

Lines 2390–92. The saying in question—*Li sanblant a son senblant trait*—is actually not recorded as such in any of the repertories of Old French proverbs, including, first of all, the well-known collection ostensibly referenced in these lines, *Li Proverbe au vilain*, edited by Adolf Tobler (1895). The traditional modern French formulation, *Qui se ressemble s'assemble*, is also absent from such thirteenth-century manuscript sources. It seems clear, however, that ascribing a proverb to *le vilain* (the peasant) is as good as saying "as people say"; in other words, no precise source is to be understood here. The proverb in question, as it happens, is ancient, going back at least as far as Homer's *Odyssey* (book 17, line 218); it is also found in Plato and, in Latin, in Cicero and Cato the Elder (among others): *Pares cum paribus [facillime] congregant.*

Line 2485. Who would be paying the high price? The French translator Micha thinks that it is the Emperor and that the narrator is speaking (Micha, *Robert le Diable*, 70). Gaucher (*Robert le Diable: Édition bilingue*) sees ambiguity, as I do. Gaucher, however, seems to view this as a bit of indirect discourse attributable to the Emperor, whereas I prefer an exclamation detached from the previous line and thus obviously and irremediably ambiguous.

Line 2612. The reference is to the legend of Saint George, saving a pagan town from a murderous dragon at the price of the inhabitants' conversion to Christianity.

Line 2825. "Far to the south": the French text specifies the Sicilian port city of Trapani.

Line 3076. The pattern of rhymed couplets in the Old French text calls here for a line rhyming with the preceding line. The omission seems to be an instance of scribal inattention, for there is no discernible break in the sense or grammatical flow of the passage from line 3075 to line 3077.

Line 3191. The banner depicting a dragon had been the standard of the Roman cavalry since the early Middle Ages.

Lines 3558–65 and 3581. These lines include allusions to two Old French proverbs, *Tant a qui chien naige* (Such is the reward for saving a drowning dog) and *De bien fait col frait* (A broken neck is the reward for a good deed), both of which express an ungrateful response to a good deed. Gaucher (*Robert le Diable: Édition bilingue*, 273) refers to Morawski, *Proverbes français*, where they are cited as numbers 2282 and 463, respectively.

Lines 3668–85. This passage, presented here in parentheses but in Löseth's edition enclosed in quotation marks, seems to be a long lament by the narrator, as seem to be a few short passages much earlier in the poem. It is notable that the pronouns, varying between *nous* and *vous*, suggest that the narrator is presenting himself as both an outsider and a citizen of Rome. Micha (*Robert le Diable*, 93–94) treats this passage simply as part of the narrative, requiring no particular punctuation or comment. Gaucher (*Robert le Diable: Édition bilingue*, lines 3300–3317) uses quotation marks, but with no explanation.

Lines 3720–25. My understanding of this passage, heavy with imperfect subjunctives, depends on my recourse to the equivalent passage in the fourteenth-century redaction of the poem: Gaucher, *Robert le Diable: Édition bilingue*, lines 3352–60.

Lines 4688–90. Pavia, capital of Lombardy, was a major city through the twelfth century and beyond. It was regarded by the anonymous Latin Goliardic poet of the time, the so-called Archpoet, as a place for a good time—perhaps with knives! Caesarea was a city in Palestine, under crusader control for most of the period from 1101 to 1265, when the conquering Mamluks demolished its walls.

Lines 4908 and 4910. The pronouns in these lines are ambiguous, but close attention to context does clarify the issue. The modern French translators Micha and Gaucher are mistaken, in my view, to attribute the Emperor's joy to the thought that it is his own status, rather than Robert's, that has been enhanced by the barons' news.

Lines 5047–78. There is no reason to accept this account of burial, interment, and sanctification as any less imaginary than the rest of the tale.

BIBLIOGRAPHY

Andries, Lise. *La Bibliothèque Bleue au dix-huitième siècle: Une tradition éditoriale*. Oxford: Voltaire Foundation, 1989.

———. "La Bibliothèque Bleue: Les réécritures de *Robert le Diable*." *Littérature* 30 (1978): 51–66. [Andries's bibliography is usefully divided under headings that can be translated as "Manuscripts and Reeditions of Manuscripts," "Incunabula," "Editions of the Seventeenth, Eighteenth, and Nineteenth Centuries," and "Critical Works of the Nineteenth and Twentieth Centuries."]

———. *Moyen Âge et colportage: Robert le Diable et autres récits*. Moyen Âge 60. Paris: Stock, 1981.

Castellani, Marie-Madeleine. "Le *Mystère de Robert le Diable* au Théâtre de la Gaîté en 1878." In Mathey-Maille and Legros, *Légende de Robert le Diable*, 235–58.

Clark, Robert. "'Le diable improbablement': *Robert le Diable* à l'Opéra de Paris." In Mathey-Maille and Legros, *Légende de Robert le Diable*, 215–34.

———. "Raising the Devil: *Robert le Diable* on the Nineteenth-Century French Stage." In *Mainte belle oeuvre faict: Études sur le théâtre médiéval offertes à Graham A. Runnalls*, edited by Denis Hüe, Mario Longtin, and Lynette Muir, 65–82. Medievalia 54. Orléans: Paradigme, 2005.

Erussard, Laurence. "The Watchdogs of the Soul: The Role of Dogs in the Spiritual Salvation of Robert the Devil." In *The Book of Nature and Humanity in the Middle Ages*, edited by David Hawkes and Richard Newhauser, 209–21. Turnhout: Brepols, 2013.

Gaspard, Claire. "Robert le Diable dans la littérature populaire (XVIIe–XIXe s)." In Mathey-Maille and Legros, *Légende de Robert le Diable*, 177–94.

Gaucher, Élisabeth, trans. and ed. *Robert le Diable: Édition bilingue français–ancien français*. Moyen Âge 17. Paris: Champion Classiques, 2006. [Gaucher's extensive bibliographies include German editions and translations, a Spanish edition and translation of 1627, and the English adaptation *Sir Gowther* (fifteenth century), with a nineteenth-century German edition of the English.]

———. *Robert le Diable: Histoire d'une légende*. Essais sur le Moyen Âge 29. Paris: Champion, 2003. [See also the informative review by Bernard Ribémont in *Cahiers de recherches médiévales et humanistes* 10 (2003), http://:crm.revues.org/224.]

Hüe, Denis. "Robert le Diable, Notre Dame et le Miracle." In Mathey-Maille and Legros, *Légende de Robert le Diable*, 43–72.

Legros, Huguette. "La folie de Robert le Diable: Réécritures et spécificités." In Mathey-Maille and Legros, *Légende de Robert le Diable*, 151–74.

Le Saux, Françoise. "Quand Robert le Diable passe Outre-Manche: *Sir Gowther*." In Mathey-Maille and Legros, *Légende de Robert le Diable*, 293–305.

Löseth, E[ilert], ed. *Robert le Diable: Roman d'Aventures*. Société des anciens textes français. Paris: Firmin Didot, 1903.

Mathey-Maille, Laurence, and Huguette Legros, eds. *La légende de Robert le Diable du Moyen Âge au XXe siècle*. Medievalia 75. Orléans: Paradigme, 2010.

Merwin, W[illiam]. S[tanley]. *Robert the Devil, Translated from an Anonymous French Play of the Fourteenth Century; with Wood-Engravings by Roxanne Sexauer*. Iowa City: Windhover Press at the University of Iowa, 1981.

Micha, Alexandre, trans. *Robert le Diable: Roman du XIIe siècle*. Paris: GF-Flammarion, 1996.

Morawski, Joseph, ed. *Proverbes français antérieurs au XVe siècle*. Classiques français du Moyen Âge 47. Paris: Champion, 1925.

Ricci, Mariagrazia. "*Robert le Diable* en prose: Les éditions du XVIe siècle." In Timelli, Ferrari, and Schoysman, *Pour un nouveau répertoire*, 245–56.

Sobczyk, Agata. "Encore un inceste occulté: L'épisode de la fille de l'empereur dans le *Roman de Robert le Diable*." *Études Médiévales* 1 (1999): 221–34.

Thompson, Stith. *Motif-Index of Folk-Literature: A Classification of Narrative Elements in Folk Tales, Ballads, Myths, Fables, Mediaeval Romances, Exempla, Fabliaux, Jest-Books, and Local Legends*. 6 vols. 1955–58. Rev. and enlarged ed. Reprint, Bloomington: Indiana University Press, 1960.

Timelli, Maria Colombo, Barbara Ferrari, and Anne Schoysman, eds. *Pour un nouveau répertoire des mises en prose*. Textes littéraires du Moyen Âge 28. Paris: Classiques Garnier, 2014.

Trocquenet, Florent. "La réécriture de *Robert le Diable* par Jean de Castilhon, ou le Moyen Âge 'raccommodé' par un écrivain en marge des Lumières." In Mathey-Maille and Legros, *Légende de Robert le Diable*, 195–214.

INDEX

All references are to line numbers.

second attack, 2551–60, 2704–10; banquet after second battle, 2763–67, 2794–98, 2851–98; Turks' third attack, 3165–68, 3534–49; banquet after third battle, 3701–4, 3736–48, 3822–932; offered to white knight, 3956–4006; at great assembly, 4105–17, 4178–87, 4245, 4257–74, 4361–63, 4421–24, 4430, 4435–89, 4757–58; speaks at the great assembly, 4490–524, 4552–615, 4643–75, 4789–815; not accepted by Robert, 4957–60

3719–73; brought before great assembly, 4725–930; choice of life as hermit, 4931–5046; disposition of his remains, 5047–78

Romaine (plain of): area near city where Turkish forces rally, 2909

Rome and Roman forces. *See headings under* Emperor of Rome

Rouen, 209, 257

Saint George (person), 2612

Saint Gilles (abbey in Nîmes), 486

Saint James (Santiago de Compostela), 487. *See also* Compostela

Saint John Lateran (church in Rome), 5056

Saint John's (church in Rome, perhaps Saint John Lateran), 511

Saint Julian (person), 760

Saint Peter (person), 2753

Saint Robert (abbey), 5077–78

Saint Robert (person). *See* Robert

Saracens (term used generically in thirteenth-century texts for Muslim forces), 1672, 1738, 1869, 1897, 1918, 2443, 2536, 2661, 2713, 2942, 3026, 3223, 3292, 3296, 3314, 3591

Satan. *See* Devil

Seine, 209

seneschal: treachery and desire for Emperor's daughter, 973–1026, 1396–437, 1505; Turks' first attack, 1550–91; Turks' second attack, 2464–83; Turks' third attack, 2993–3010; prepares to pass for the white knight, 4007–77; at great assembly, 4129–489; escape, 4525–46, 4612–20

Turkish fighters and allies: Alexandria, 2927; Anatolia, 1515; Arabs/Arabia, 2450; Asia Minor, 1439, 1996; Babylon (in Egypt), 2918; Babylon (in the desert), 2916; Camela, 2929; Caspian Alans, 1995; Caspian coast, 1440, 1516, 2932, 2938; Caspian Comans, 2450; Damascus, 2930; Edessa, 2932; Khorasan (including its king), 1440, 1516, 1957, 1961, 2451, 2933; Macedonia, 2918; Moors (king of the), 3232; Nirvana (city), 2452; Romaine, 2997; Rus, 2928; Spain, 2928; Syria, 2923; Turkmens, 1995. *See also* Saracens

Turks: first attack on Rome, 1439–2033; aftermath of first attack, 2089–106; second attack on Rome, 2409–62, 2503–679; third attack on Rome, 2903–3406

Valona (in Albania): site of a rally for Turkish forces, 2926

Printed in the United States
By Bookmasters